Who is Carl?

Carl Goes is named after an old friend with wanderlust who died too young. Carl was an avid collector of travel guides from the 1800s, a time in which a global standard for travel books was set.

Our friend Carl had only debts when he passed away, so everything he owned had to be sold at auction. We decided to pool our money and buy back everything we knew he loved — some antique paintings, family jewellery, and of course, his beloved travel book collection. Remarkably, when the antique traders in the room realised we were the friends and family of our dear friend, they stopped bidding, helping us save everything we could.

We wanted to pay tribute to our friend Carl by creating a modern-day series of books encapsulating a new type of travel, where work, play, creativity and curiosity combine. Capturing the spirit of the man *Carl Goes* is named after, our guides are for all the curious and creative folks on the planet. We hope Carl would be proud.

Foreword

Welcome to *Carl Goes Kassel*, a book that brings local voices to our entrepreneurial, creative and generally curious readers.

Kassel is a city with a beating heart that peaks every five years when the world famous *documenta* exhibition of modern and contemporary art arrives. The 100-day festival sees the city transformed, with art installations and events springing up across Kassel. The population of the city swells, with up to a million of the world's art lovers arriving, giving Kassel an uber-international personality.

While *documenta* provides a cultural structure, the city has a thriving creative and entrepreneurial scene every other day of the year too. The Art University Kassel (Kunsthochschule Kassel) has a big influence, with former students setting up creative enterprises that rival those in much larger cities. In tech, entrepreneurial start-up businesses congregate in the Science Park. And across the city, creativity and entrepreneurialism collide in innovative businesses, whether its upcycling fashion, quirky museums or craft beers brewed with the city's honey.

Some call Kassel 'the forest with a few houses', embodying a feeling that is often more 'green' and less 'city'. So it's no wonder that during their leisure time, Kasselaners love to chill out in the city's parks, including in Bergpark Wilhelmshöhe, a UNESCO World Heritage Site and the largest hillside park in Europe. During summer the outdoors takes on a new meaning, with some brave locals reinstating the former trend of river bathing.

With a feeling of space, creative freedom and influence from the art world's greats, we invite you to become a citizen of Kassel for the time being.

Sascha Mengerink, Publisher
Sasha Arms, Editor

Contents

Orangerie at Karlsaue Park. Photo: Jörg Conrad. © Stadt Kassel

Man Walking to the Sky. © Stadt Kassel/Michael Schwab

Lake Buga at the Fulda river. Photo: Weber Fotografie Kassel. © Stadt Kassel

Kassel's DNA

A visual tour of Kassel's identity.

Office of Stephan Haberzettl © Stephan Haberzettl

1. Green, green green – a city more like a forest with a few houses.
2. Leftover *documenta* artworks and installations.
3. The Fulda river, where locals love to go bathing and boating in the summer.
4. Collaboration – people come together in small offices so they don't have to work alone.
5. But people live alone, since it's a city of more space, freedom and cheaper rents than other cities.
6. Hilly residential roads – like the San Francisco of Germany!
7. Fitness centres and gyms are everywhere...

South Kassel © Stadt Kassel/Martina Eull

Obere Königsstrasse Photo: Weber Fotografie Kassel. © Stadt Kassel

Three days in Kassel

Get a feeling for the city and join Kasselaners doing the things they love best during three fun-packed days.

Day one
Spend your first day in Kassel checking out the city centre. Nothing is too far away in this city, so the best way to explore is on foot. Check out Königsplatz and the side streets around it, then pop into the Fridericianum (p52) to enjoy contemporary art in one of Europe's oldest museums. Stop for lunch at Take Hallali Burger (p50), a local institution, before taking a stroll around Karlsaue Park (p53) and along the Fulda river (p52). Experience some of Kassel's quirkier side by stopping off at the Museum of Sepulchral Culture (p11), then take a tour of the air-raid shelter in Weinberg (p14). Have a Vietnamese dinner at the locals' current favourite, Pho Vang (p49), then head for a quiet drink in the beer garden at Rondell (p51).

Day two
Get an overview of Kassel's neighbourhoods through Kassel Greeters (www.kasselgreeters.de), where Kassel locals show off their city free of charge. Alternatively, take a self-guided tour on the number one tram, which travels from the north to the west of the city via the centre. Get off in the area around Mombachstrasse to get a feeling of student life. Stop for a cheap coffee at Cafeteria Pavillon (p50), see entrepreneurs at work at the bicycle repair shop and café, Fahrradwerkstatt und Café DesAStA (p50), then have lunch in the low key Turkish restaurant, Restaurant Lehmofen (p50). In the afternoon, head up to the end of the line at Bergpark Wilhelmshöhe (p52), the UNESCO World Heritage Site and the largest hillside park in Europe. See the famous Hercules statue, stop for a drink at Café Jérôme (p29) and then spend some down time at the thermal baths, Kurhessen Therme (p53). In the evening, enjoy the quaint surroundings of Lange Strasse during a meal at the traditional Brauhaus Zum Rammelsberg (p51), then take in an independent film at the Gloria cinema (p52), where everything is decorated in green.

Day three
Most locals consider the Vorderer Westen neighbourhood to be the most interesting and beautiful, so spend the day there soaking up the atmosphere. Have coffee at the roastery, Seegert Kaffeerösterei (p51), buy original illustrated books at Rotopol (p52) and find gifts at the Wildwood Gallery & Store (p52). After a slow food, vegetarian lunch at Bashis Delight (p49), continue exploring the area by taking in the impressive Kongress Palais, and stopping for a glass of wine in Chacal (p51). On your last evening in Kassel, treat yourself to a meal in the Spanish El Erni (p49) or the traditional German denkMAHL (p49). Hang out with the locals in the evening at King Schulz bar (p51).

Three weeks in Kassel

Become a local in different neighbourhoods and get to know some creative entrepreneurs.

Week one
Since Kassel is a city of art, spend your first week soaking up the city's inherent creativity. There are still plenty of installations from previous *documenta* exhibitions to be found across the city. These include the bronze sculpture of a leafless tree, *The Vertical Earth Kilometer* by Walter de Maria on Friedrichsplatz (p53); the *Rahmenbau* giant picture frame that forms a window to Karlsaue Park and the landscape beyond by Haus-Rucker-Co; and *Pickaxe* on the riverbanks of the Fulda. Stop by St. Martin's Church (Martinskirche) to see the largest organ in Europe, with a metre of hair hanging over it (p53). Weave in some of the alternative creative sights of Kassel too, including the brutalist Art University Kassel (Kunsthochschule Kassel) on the edge of the Karlsaue Park (p53). Check out the programme at Tokonoma (p53), the platform for young art in the city, and visit the events and exhibitions at Kunsttempel (p53), Kasseler Kunstverein (p53) and Neue Galerie (p53). Spend evenings at creative food events, such as the ones by Stulle & Gut (p50), and watch performances at the Staatstheater (p53) and SOZO visions in motions dance company (p53).

Week two
After getting an idea of the art credentials of the city during week one, spend your remaining time getting to know the rhythms of the different neighbourhoods in Kassel. The centre is an obvious hive of activity, although green space is never too far away either. Take advantage of the shops (and free Wi-Fi) of City Point (p29), understand Kassel through its museums such as GRIMMWELT (p34) about the Brothers Grimm, and enjoy foodie pit stops at Avanti (p49), Hans Wurst (p49) and Namaste (p49). Stop for coffee and people-watching at ALEX (p50) and spend fun evenings in Fes Musikbar (p51). Enjoy the south of the city too, with long walks in Karlsaue Park (p53) and Fuldaaue (p52). Revel in the distinctly arty feeling that spills over from Art University Kassel, particularly at Weinberg Corner (p55).

Week three
Spend your final week in two of the most vibrant parts of Kassel: the north and the west. Soak up the feeling of internationalism, entrepreneurship and student innovation in the north, by wandering around the area near the Science Park (p26). Enjoy delicious Ethiopian and Turkish meals at Abessina (p49) or Café Bistro Hurricane (p49), and spend evenings at Goldgrube Kassel (p53) for live music and Mutter (p51) for drinks. In the west, enjoy wandering and exploring the prettiest part of the city. Have a low-key coffee at Café Buch-Oase (p50) and Melchior Coffee (p50), and shop for fine alcoholic beverages at Weinhandlung Bremer (p52). Enjoy discovering the small shops around Friedrich-Ebert-Strasse (p52), and in the evenings, sample fresh flavours at Heimat (p49), Sapori D'Italia (p50) and Shinyu Sushi House (p50). You'll feel like a true Kassel local by the end of your stay.

Carmen José
Illustrator

This illustrator and creative entrepreneur moved from Madrid to Kassel after falling in love with the city's Art University Kassel (Kunsthochschule Kassel). Carmen is the co-founder of Papiercafé, a café and bookshop for self-published student titles, and a venue for some *documenta* events. In addition, Carmen co-manages Rotopol, a publishing house, gallery and shop for graphic storytelling, which is also home to her illustration studio.

Introduce yourself.
I was born in Valencia and grew up in Madrid. My parents have always worked in the art field, taking my sisters and I to galleries every weekend. They always encouraged us to be creative, so it was a natural step for me to get into art. I studied Fine Art in Madrid, which involved all the classical areas of art: painting, sculpting and natural drawing with charcoal. After two years, I wanted a new perspective, so I applied for an Erasmus exchange, and ended up in Art University Kassel in 2011, just before *documenta 13*.

What is Art University Kassel like?
It has an amazingly open structure and students have the freedom to try anything. I liked it so much I decided to stay to finish my degree. All the professors are also artists, so they have real experiences to share. After becoming interested in illustration, I had the opportunity to work as an assistant to illustration artist Professor Hendrik Dorgathen, which was another incredible opportunity.

Tell us about Papiercafé.
Myself and Kathi Seemann – a good friend and photographer – both love mixed book and coffee shop concepts, where people meet friends and share ideas. They're not very common in Germany, so we decided to start Papiercafé. It began as a pop-up shop during the Art University Kassel's summer exhibition, the Rundgang. We served coffee and sold self-published books by students from the university. We also popped up in Tokonoma, a platform in Kassel for young art, and Kunsttempel, a literary house. Then we found a longer-term space for Papiercafé at the university. We run events too, including discussions with artists, film screenings and we host some *documenta* sessions.

Describe the book you produced for your university 'master project', *THERE : HERE (ALLÍ : HIER)*.
I'm interested in people who are living between places, like me. I feel I have homes in Spain and Germany, but I don't belong in either. The open migration opportunities across Europe and mass migration caused by crises in other countries is a modern experience. Even in Spain, many young people leave to find better jobs elsewhere. For my book, I started collecting these different feelings and thinking about them in a visual way.

Tell us about your work at Rotopol.
Rotopol was set up by a group of friends from Art University Kassel just before *documenta 12*. Rita Fürstenau, who still runs Rotopol, was looking for someone to manage it with her. I've been a fan of Rotopol since arriving in Kassel, so it was a great opportunity. Now I have my illustration studio there, I work with all our illustrators and I travel to festivals across the world to promote our work. At the moment, we're planning some of our visits to Leipzig, Lucerne and Toronto.

What does your future hold?
There are many opportunities in Kassel for artists, particularly because of *documenta*. But it's important to get new inspiration, so I'd like to do an artist residency in another country in the future. I'm really interested in Japanese culture and I'm learning the language, so I may go to Japan. In the creative world, you can't plan too much. It's good to keep things open, make connections and take chances.

What's life like for creative people in Kassel?
It's like a family: everyone knows each other and we often end up at the same parties and exhibitions. Kassel is better for keeping focused than larger cities. The parks help; walking in Karlsaue Park calms me and frees my mind. Across the river, the Fuldaaue is full of forested areas and lakes, which is very peaceful too. When

I was in Madrid, the always on culture made it difficult to concentrate. Kassel is a great place to have your creative headquarters, and so many cities in Europe are easily accessible.

Which Kassel neighbourhood do you live in?

I've always lived in the south because of the Art University Kassel; it's where I feel at home. It's a quiet neighbourhood full of art students and families. I used to have a flat share and now I live alone because Kassel is cheap compared to other cities. The south is all about the connection to Art University Kassel and the Karlsaue Park. I love the cafés and galleries in the neighbourhood, which often do openings together as mini-festivals. I've discovered first-hand that you can stay for weeks in the south without going anywhere else in the city!

Where do you go for inspiration?

My favourite place is the Fulda river. Kassel is recovering an old tradition of river swimming and I swim there very often in the summer. Whenever I'm stuck on a piece of work, sitting on the wharf of one of the canoe clubs along the river is inspiring and helps with dynamic thinking.

What smell do you associate with Kassel?

Wet earth on a rainy day.

Where do you go for some laptop time?

I love working at Kafe NEU am Weinberg in the south. As well as laptop working and meetings, it's good for the open mic nights. I really like Kollektivcafé Kurbad near the east, which is also Kassel's bathtub museum, Kurbad Jungborn! It's on the river and you can sit outside in the summer. They also host political talks and concerts. I find the north of Kassel very interesting because all the students are there; Café DesAStA is a good student-run café. In the west, I like Café Buch-Oase.

What's the Kassel vibe when *documenta* is on?

It feels different, with so many people to connect with and inspiring things going on every day. *documenta* is paradise for artists and art students. I particularly enjoyed *documenta 13* because a lot of it took place in the parks. My favourite was *FOREST (for a thousand years)*, a 3D sound installation by Cardiff and Miller. I also liked *Trail* by Natascha Sadr Haghighian, a footpath connecting Bellevue and Karlsaue Park. I also worked for one of the *documenta* artists, Dora García, helping with her *Klau Mich Show*, a TV and performance project about radicalism in society.

Which is your favourite *documenta* installation of all time?

7000 Oaks by Joseph Beuys from *documenta 7*. Beuys planted 7,000 oak trees across Kassel. It's not just art; it's a political act. Whenever you go somewhere in Kassel, you see the trees and realise what a lasting legacy it will have.

Where are your favourite places to eat out in Kassel?

My current favourite is NACHBAR, which is a burger place using high quality meat from the region. It's so popular, you need a reservation. There's a sushi place I really like in the west called Sushi Bar. You have to walk a little to get there, but it's worth it. Also in the centre is a great Vietnamese restaurant called Pho Vang. There's an Ethiopian restaurant I really like in north Kassel, called Abessina. Stulle & Gut is a catering project run by good friends, so I like eating at their events too.

What do you like doing in the evening?

Weinbergkrug is my favourite bar in the south. After a day's work at Rotopol in the west, Chacal has an authentic French atmosphere for a glass of wine. In the north, Mutter is a really fun bar. My favourite beer garden is Rondell, which has a perfect view of the river. For entertainment, Theaterstübchen is a great venue; I especially like their jazz concerts. For films, Kassel has three independent cinemas: Bali, Filmladen and my favourite, Gloria, where everything is decorated in green! Kulturzentrum Schlachthof is a cultural centre on the site of a former slaughterhouse with an interesting programme of events. And lastly, Kassel has a prominent modern dance culture that I really like, especially the work of choreographer Johannes Wieland and the SOZO visions in motion dance company.

Where are your favourite shops in Kassel?

I love WIKULLiL, which supplies materials for creative people in the city. I also worked there for a year and I like it for paper, Japanese-made items and great advice from the owner. Antiquariat & Verlag Winfried Jenior is my favourite second-hand book shop.

What is the current trend in Kassel?

Anything organic, handmade and back-to-local is trending. There are a lot of new shops and bio-supermarkets (biomarkts) opening capturing this ethos. Kasselaners really appreciate it.

How would you advise visitors to Kassel to blend in and live like locals?

Explore other neighbourhoods away from the centre and during *documenta*, don't just go to the official locations. Try to get a little lost too.

What music is on your soundtrack to Kassel?

Robin & The Elephant, an indie pop band I like watching live. One of the musicians is a friend from the Art University Kassel and the music suits Kassel perfectly.

What is Kassel's best quality?

At the weekend, it's normal for locals to walk in the forest or go to their garden (kleingarten). People are very connected to nature. Kassel's daily rhythm is a little slower because of its green parts.

Find out more about Carmen José at www.carmenjose.com

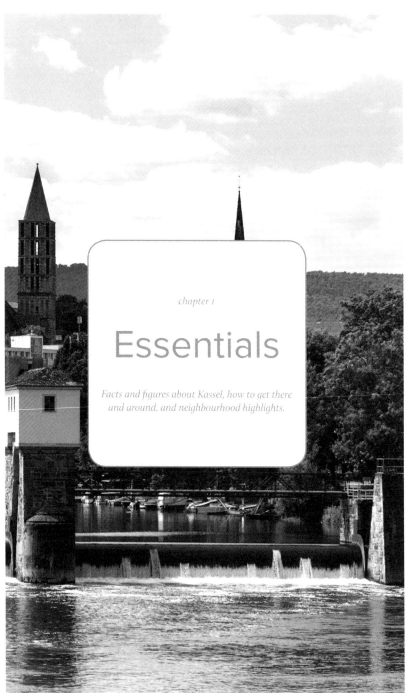

chapter 1

Essentials

*Facts and figures about Kassel, how to get there
and around, and neighbourhood highlights.*

Facts and figures

Currency
Euro (€)

Customs
Visit the Zoll website for information: www.zoll.de

Electricity
220 volts, Schuko plug or Europlug

Geographical location
51.31° N and 9.48° E

Language
German

Local time
Central European Time (CET) / Central European Summer Time (CEST)

Postal code
34001–34134

Tax
19% VAT is added to most items for sale in Germany. For items that cost more than €25, non-residents can claim a VAT refund. Visit the Global Blue website for more information:
www.globalblue.com

Telephone country code
+49

Telephone area code
561

Tipping
Add 5-10% on top of restaurant bills for service

Visas
Not required for EU nationals. Some non-EU nationals do not need a visa for visits of up to 90 days; other non-EU nationals need a visa. See Germany's Federal Foreign Office website for more information about visa requirements:
www.auswaertiges-amt.de

Important phone numbers
Police: 110
Ambulance or fire department: 112

Etiquette
Some people in Kassel speak English, but not as many as in larger cities such as Berlin. Regardless, it pays to be polite and ask if someone speaks English ('Sprechen Sie Englisch?') before assuming they do.

Good time-keeping is important in Kassel: be on time for appointments, whether they are formal or social. Address people formally with a Mr (Herr) or Mrs (Frau) preceding their surname, until asked to do otherwise.

Greet people by saying 'Guten Tag' or the less formal 'Hallo'. Say goodbye with 'Auf Wiedersehen' or the less formal 'tschüss'.

Useful websites
Kassel Marketing:
www.kassel-marketing.de
Stadtportal Kassel:
www.kassel.de

Neue Galerie. Photo: Michael Schwab. © Stadt Kassel

Interesting facts:
- World famous for: *documenta* art exhibition, held every five years
- Population: +200,000
- Population during *documenta*: 1 million
- Size of city: 107 km²
- Students: +23,000

- Home to the biggest hillside park in Europe: Bergpark Wilhelmshöhe, 2.4km²
- Claim to fame: home of the Brothers Grimm
- Kassel is the home of several quirky museums, including: the Museum of Sepulchral

Culture which focuses on tombs and death, the German Wallpaper Museum and the Kassel Bath Museum, Kurbad Jungborn.

www.sepulkralmuseum.de
www.hlmd.de
www.kurbad-jungborn.de

7,000 oak trees 🌳 were planted in Kassel in 1982 for *documenta 7* 90% of the city centre was rebuilt during the 1950s following wartime bombing 🧨 raids The *Transformer* 🤖 *Statue*, designed by a Chinese artist, was brought to Kassel for the world premiere of the *Transformers* film in 2012 *documenta* attracts the rich and famous as well as art heroes. This includes Brad Pitt, who attended *documenta* 13 Kassel has been illuminated by laser beams 📐 during weekend nights, since *documenta 6* in 1977 Kassel is the home of several quirky museums, including the Kassel Bath 🛁 Museum The Ottoneum in Kassel 🏛 was the first permanent theatre built in Germany in 1605. It's now a museum of natural history Bruce Willis's 🧍 mother comes from Kassel *The Illogic of Kassel* is a semi-fictional book 📖 written by celebrated Spanish author Enrique Vila-Matas. He was invited to sit in a window of a Chinese greasy spoon during *documenta* one year, as a writer in residence art installation for the exhibition Around 70% of German Apfelwein production is consumed in Hessen, the region Kassel is located in. Every Hessian drinks 10 litres of Apfelwein 🍷 per year, compared to the 1.2 litres drunk by Germans living in other regions Hessen is the economically strongest state in Germany, with the 🪙 highest GDP Items shipped from North Hessen can reach any destination in Germany by road within 5 hours 🚚 2 million people in Hessen do volunteering There are 3,500 choirs 🏘 and 110,000 singers in Hessen

Getting there

By air

Kassel Calden Airport (KSF)
Kassel's airport is a minor international airport, located 16km north west of Kassel. There are just a few direct flights into and out of the airport each week. Travellers arriving at the airport can travel to Kassel via the number 100 bus, which takes approximately 40 minutes and costs €3,70.

Many travellers find it more convenient to fly into a larger airport in surrounding cities and catch the train to Kassel. The most convenient airports are:

Hannover Airport (HAJ)
From the airport, take the S5 train to Hannover train station, which takes approximately 20 minutes. Then take the high-speed Intercity-Express (ICE) train, which takes an hour to reach Kassel.

Frankfurt am Main International Airport (FRA)
From the airport, take an ICE or S5 train to Frankfurt train station, which takes approximately 15 minutes. Then take the high-speed ICE train, which takes an hour and 25 minutes to reach Kassel.

Paderborn Lippstadt Airport (PAD)
From the airport, catch the BahnBusHochstift (BBH) bus shuttle line S60 or 460 to Paderborn rail station. From there, take a local or ICE train service to Kassel, with a journey time of approximately one hour.

The one-way journey price to Kassel from any of these airports starts from €19 but can be much more expensive, depending on the time of travel and whether tickets are purchased in advance.
reiseauskunft.bahn.de

By train
A number of long distance trains pass through Kassel-Wilhelmshöhe train station. Destinations from which Kassel can be easily reached via these services include Basel, Berlin, Dresden, Düsseldorf, Frankfurt, Hamburg, Hannover, Leipzig, Munich and Stuttgart.

Getting around

Public transport
Kassel's public transport system consists of trams, buses and trains. Visitors staying in most hotels in the city will receive a free MeineCard, allowing travel on all public transport for the duration of the visit. Alternatively, a short distance (kurzstrecke) ticket, valid for up to 4 stops on trams and buses, or up to 3km on trains, costs €1,60. A single trip ticket (einzelfahrkarte) for longer distances costs €2,80, or €3,70 if you're travelling into the Kassel suburbs. MultiTickets are also available for €7, which last for 24 hours or a whole weekend. For groups of people, up to five people can travel together for the same period of time on a standard MultiTicket, which costs €8,90.

Note: most Kassel locals refer to trams as 'trains'!

Check the KVG (Kasseler Verkehrs-Gesellschaft Aktiengesellschaft) website for information about tickets and public transport routes.

An app, NVV Mobil, is also available to download, which shows real-time information about travel routes.
www.kvg.de

Those planning on visiting attractions and participating in the walking tours run by Kassel Marketing may find a KasselCard or a MeineCardPlus better value for money.
www.kassel-marketing.de
www.meinecardplus.nordhessen.de

Bicycle
Konrad is Kassel's city cycling scheme, with more than 50 rental stations and 500 bicycles available across the city. Register as a customer first, either online or at one of the main Konrad terminals (available at Kassel or Kassel-Wilhelmshöhe train stations, or Friedrichsplatz). Then rent a bike at any rental station by calling the phone number written on the bicycle you want to rent, which will recognise your phone number and unlock the bike. It costs €1 per hour to rent a bicycle, with a maximum charge of €10 over 24 hours.
www.konrad-kassel.de

Neighbourhoods

A flavour of Kassel's localities.

Centre
The centre of Kassel is home to the city's best known institutions, including the Fridericianum contemporary art museum (the oldest museum to be built in Europe) and Staatstheater Kassel. This area is also the centre of *documenta* every five years. Even in the centre of Kassel you're just a stone's throw from greenery: the Karlsaue Park and Orangerie can be accessed via a stunning approach behind the *documenta* hall.

Recommended by locals:

Stellwerk Kassel
This gallery run by students from the Art University Kassel can be found at the rail station, making the experience of train travel a little more creative.
Rainer-Dierichs-Platz 1, 34117
Facebook @stellwerk
Train: Kassel Hauptbahnhof

North
The northern part of Kassel is thronging with activity, thanks to the student population from the University of Kassel. This makes it a centre of innovation too, with start-ups – particularly in tech – congregating at the Science Park. There's also a thriving international population, with residents from across the world living in the area.

Recommended by locals:

Fahrradwerkstatt und Café DesAStA
This student initiative is described by locals to have a hippy-like, political flavour.

While the café is a cool meeting place for discussions over coffee, the attached bicycle workshop is a place where students can learn how to fix their bikes.
Arnold Bode Strasse 6, 34127
Facebook
@KaffeTrinkenImDesasta
Tram: Holländischer Platz/
Universität

South
The southern part of Kassel is characterised by the Art University Kassel and the green expanses. It's an area to explore small creative enterprises, visit miniature art galleries, and be inspired amid the greenery. The brutalist, Bauhaus architecture of the Art University Kassel is a surprise to some, but students love it for the baseline it gives them in comparison to the creativity that lies within.

Recommended by locals:

Air-raid shelter in Weinberg
Used to store ice and beer in the early 19th century, this area was subsequently an air raid shelter for 7,500 people in the 1930s, complete with a medical area, emergency room and military command section. Guided tours reveal the bunker is largely unchanged, except for damage from an illegal techno party in 1992.
Weinbergstrasse, 34117
+49 (0)175 286 5617
Tram: Am Weinberg

East
This area of the city is the quiet part, home to small, light industry and a thrumming residential population who enjoy a peaceful existence. Peppered with modern architecture, it's also not a bad-looking part of the city either, bringing up

the standards from the less impressive post-war era.

Recommended by locals:

craftBEE
This craft beer maker creates beer using Kassel honey. The beer is made in the east of the city and can be found in various bars across Kassel.
Schwanenweg 19a, 34123
+49 (0)162 175 6682
info@craftbee.de
www.craftbee.de
Tram: Hallenbad Ost

West
The west of Kassel was the least damaged part during the war, and with its traditional red brick buildings, it's widely considered to be the most beautiful area today. The Vorderer Westen neighbourhood is the most popular, with well-regarded creative enterprises, antiques shops and art galleries. This centres on and around Friedrich-Ebert-Strasse which has won several prizes for its boulevard-like revival. Further west is Bergpark Wilhelmshöhe, the widely adored UNESCO World Heritage hillside park.

Recommended by locals:

LAGE and Galerie Coucou
Kassel's art scenesters flock to these galleries every time there's a new showing.
Elfbuchenstrasse 20, 34119
hi@lage-kassel.de
www.lage-kassel.de
+49 (0)170 969 9897
info@coucou-coucou.com
www.coucou-coucou.com
Tram: Friedenskirche

Fridericianum Photo: Stephan Kaiser © Stadt Kassel

University of Kassel. Photo: Weber Fotografie Kassel. © Stadt Kassel

Karlsaue. Photo: Jörg Conrad. © Stadt Kassel

South Kassel, seen from the Weinberg Photo: Martina Eull © Stadt Kassel

Photo: craftBEE

Wilhelmshöhe. Photo: Tobias Gründer. © Stadt Kassel

Kassel's neighbourhoods

1. Fridericianum in the centre of Kassel.
2. University of Kassel, north Kassel.
3. Karlsaue Park and Orangerie in the centre of Kassel.
4. South Kassel seen from the Weinberg.
5. craftBEE beer made with Kassel honey in the east of Kassel.
6. Bergpark Wilhelmshöhe, west Kassel.

A work day in Kassel:

Morning

Science Park
Spend some time in the co-working space of this start-up hub and have a coffee with entrepreneurs in The Science Lounge. Page 26.

Kulturzentrum Schlachthof
Stop by this cultural centre on the site of a former slaughterhouse to check out the creative events. Page 53.

Falada
Have a business lunch using locally-sourced produce in a Scandi-style interior, overlooking lush greenery. Page 34.

Afternoon

WIKULLiL
Gain some creative inspiration in this shop known for visionary stationery supplies. Page 52.

Papiercafé
Have some coffee and laptop time in this space for self-published books inside the art academy, Art University Kassel (Kunsthochschule Kassel). Page 50.

Kurbad Jungborn
Enjoy the creative spark of Kassel's quirky bathtub museum, and sit in the adjoining Kollektivcafé Kurbad. Page 53.

Evening

Orangerie
Have a post-work drink in beautiful park-side surroundings while checking emails on the free Wi-Fi. Page 51.

Voit
Impress business associates with a meal in this fine dining restaurant, complete with design details by Kassel designers Aust & Amelung. Page 50.

Casa Colombiana
This bar runs an after-work party for local business people every few months. Check it out to rub shoulders with local entrepreneurs. Page 51.

A day of play in Kassel:

Morning

KulturBahnhof
Check out the area around Kassel train station which is an artistic and cultural hub. Page 54.

Rokkeberg Coffee & Juice
Have a pit stop at this locally loved café for coffee, juice or cake. Page 50.

Markthalle Kassel
Wander around this foodie hub in the pretty market hall, and have an early lunch at one of the food stands. Page 49.

Afternoon

Friedrich-Ebert-Strasse
Wander along this award-winning street for antiques and boutique stores. Page 52.

soki
Have a look around this upcycling shop, with original handmade fashions crafted from pre-loved materials. Page 52.

LAGE and Galerie Coucou
Check out the latest art at these galleries frequented by the art scenesters of Kassel. Page 53.

Evening

craftBEE
Enjoy an early-evening drink of this local beer made with city honey. Page 14.

NACHBAR
Sate your appetite with a low-key dinner at one of the best burger bars in town. Page 49.

Weinberg Corner
Check out one of the spaces at Weinberg Corner, where art, live music and creative readings are the order of the day. Page 55.

Events and key dates

An outline of national holidays and popular events, as well as quirky and vibrant festivals in Kassel.

Spring

- Good Friday and Easter Monday: national holidays
- 1 May: national holiday (Workers' Day)
- Ascension Day: national holiday

documenta
This world-famous, 100-day exhibition of contemporary art dates back to 1955, and takes place in Kassel every five years. Attracting high-profile artists and art fans from across the globe, Kassel's population swells to five times its usual size. The city becomes the artist's canvas, and many sculptures and artworks can be found across the city from previous *documenta* exhibitions.
www.documenta.de

Bergpark-Konzerte
Open-air music performances covering multiple genres take place in the stunning surroundings of Bergpark Wilhelmshöhe every year.
www.bergpark-konzerte.de

Fotobookfestival Kassel
The annual festival is a forum on photography books. There are artist lectures, book exhibitions and booksellers showcasing photography books. It also involves a competition for the best unpublished photobook mock-up, with winners gaining a publishing contract.
www.fotobookfestival.org

Kultursommer Nordhessen
This annual cultural event plays host to concerts in unusual venues across the region, from orchestral concerts in barns to jazz in the forest.
www.kultursommer-nordhessen.de

Day of Architecture
This annual day sees interesting buildings not usually open to the public, open their doors and invite guests in.
www.tag-der-architektur.de

Summer

- Pentecost (Whitsun): national holiday

Party on the Fulda
This party on the river every summer is a chance for outdoor fun for all Kasselaners, and is closely followed by the City of Kassel's annual birthday party celebrations.

Kunsthochschule Kassel Rundgang
Art University Kassel opens its doors for a week every summer for the students' final presentation of the year. Visitors can access workrooms and exhibition spaces, and are treated to various artistic works, from fine art to visual communication. There are also tours, open air film screenings and lectures.
www.kunsthochschulekassel.de

Installation in the documenta archive © Stadt Kassel. Photo: Harry Soremski

Kulturzelt
This annual festival is all about music, attracting an eclectic blend of music-lovers from across the world. There are events for every kind of music, from jazz to electronic dancehall.
www.kulturzelt-kassel.de

Brothers Grimm Festival
This summer festival celebrates Kassel's history with the Brothers Grimm, involving a range of events for families and fairy-tale-lovers.
www.brueder-grimm-festival.com

Autumn

- 3 October: national holiday (German Unity Day)

Kassel Marathon
This annual run takes a route around some of the best sights in Kassel.
www.kassel-marathon.de

Connichi
Germany's biggest anime convention takes place in Kassel every year, attracting more than 20,000 people, who dress up as their favourite anime characters.
www.connichi.de

Atelierrundgang
Kassel artists open their ateliers for a weekend to give visitors a behind-the-scenes look. A range of exhibitions, workshops and performances take place, which proves fascinating for anyone with an interest in the arts.
www.atelierrundgang.net

Kassel Dokfest
This annual documentary film and video festival involves the showing of 300 films and various cinematic events.
www.kasselerdokfest.de

Startup School
Kassel's start-up school is run out of the University of Kassel. The programme involves workshops throughout the year on diverse aspects of starting a business.
www.uni-kassel.de/ukt/unikat/startup-school

Freeflow Festival
This festival is about improvised arts, with a range of performances and exhibits.
www.freeflowfestival.de

Kasseler Jazzfest
This annual festival involves jazz sessions, performances and workshops, attracting local and global jazz lovers.
www.jazzvereinkassel.de

Kasseler Museumsnacht
For one evening a year, dozens of Kassel museums and cultural institutions open their doors to offer unique experiences, including tours, readings and performances.
www.museumsnacht.de

Kasseler Musiktage
One of the oldest and most famous music festivals in Europe, numerous concerts are held for chamber music and orchestral compositions.
www.kasseler-musiktage.de

OHRENKRATZER Kooperative für Neue Musik
This collective for women's music involves performances of improvised music.
www.ohrenkratzer.de

Day of Monuments
For one day a year, historic buildings and monuments which are not usually open to the public, open their doors and allow visitors to explore.
tag-des-offenen-denkmals.de

Winter

- 24 to 26 December: national holiday (Christmas)
- 1 January: national holiday (New Year's Day)

Graphic Novel Festival
This festival looks at current trends in graphic novels and comics, involving exhibitions and global experts.
www.festival-geks.de

Soundcheck im Eulensaal
This contemporary concert project involves performances in a combination of spoken word, music and other artistic disciplines, designed to spark intellectual debate.
www.soundcheck-kassel.de

Other events

Kassel's various museums, institutions and venues have diverse calendars of events and exhibitions from year to year. Here are some of our favourites:

Fridericianum
One of Europe's oldest public museums, dedicated to contemporary art.
www.fridericianum.org

Messe Kassel
National and international fairs take place at this large exhibition space every year.
www.messe-kassel.de

Kongress Palais Kassel
An impressive building of neoclassical architecture which hosts events and artistic performances.
www.kongress-palais.de

Useful websites:
Kassel Stadtportal
www.kassel.de
Eventful
www.eventful.com/kassel/events
EVENTIM
www.eventim.de/kassel

Susanne Pfeffer

Director of Museum Fridericianum

Curator and art historian Susanne Pfeffer is a global name in the art world. She has curated hundreds of exhibitions for well-known museums and artists, and since 2013, Susanne has been heading up the Fridericianum—one of the oldest public museums in Europe. She is also regularly invited to curate exhibitions at major art festivals across the world, including the Venice Biennale, and has advised institutions such as MoMA PS1.

Tell us about your background.
I studied art history at the Humboldt University of Berlin and went into contemporary art because I found it exciting to work in the 'now', reflecting the urgent questions of our times. I like working directly with artists and realising exhibitions and projects together with them. I worked at the Kölnischer Kunstverein in Cologne and the Museum für Moderne Kunst in Frankfurt am Main before taking the position of Artistic Director at the Künstlerhaus Bremen. Following that, I was curator at Kunst-Werke in Berlin for several years, and I also advised and curated exhibitions for other institutions including the Museion in Bolzano and MoMA PS1 in New York. In 2013, I became the Director of the Fridericianum.

Did you always know you would go into art?
I was always interested in art, but also in literature, philosophy, theatre, and cinema. In time, I realised that my way of thinking is quite visual; it's outside the boundaries of language. In a way, that's a good match for working with artists.

What are you doing to keep the Fridericianum relevant today?
The Fridericianum was the first museum to be built, in 1779, so the spirit of modernity is inherently present in it. I understand the Fridericianum as a place for discourse; a place to explore and debate socially relevant issues. Art can reflect the radical changes that we are currently experiencing: our bodies and lives are metamorphosing under the influence of technology. We can no longer make a distinction between nature and culture. The group exhibitions *Speculations on Anonymous Materials, nature after nature*, and *Inhuman* brought together artists working on these concerns. For each of these exhibitions, we hosted symposiums with international philosophers to think through the issues at stake. One of our recent symposiums was committed to questioning how new forms of fascism are emerging all over the globe. Exhibitions at the Fridericianum feature young artists, who often produce new works for the Fridericianum, but we also have retrospectives of older artists such as Marcel Broodthaers, Tetsumi Kudo, and Paul Sharits, whose works are still, or perhaps more than ever, relevant and urgent for understanding our time.

What's the best thing about your job?
The Fridericianum gives me a lot of freedom and allows me to be hands-on with exhibitions; I feel that this is quite remarkable. For me, it is the best place to work I can imagine.

What is it like to work in the art field in Kassel?
It's very concentrated and every encounter is really personal. Since Kassel is so well-known for contemporary art, it's easy to convince people to come here to work on projects together. When we're doing group exhibitions, the participating artists join us in Kassel for the installation. The whole experience is more personal and profound. In larger cities, people in this situation would have a tendency to work and socialise less as a group.

How does Kassel feel when *documenta* is on?
It's beautiful that so many people come to Kassel with the sole purpose of looking at art, thinking about art, and discussing art. It can feel quite overwhelming; people come together from across the world. The Fridericianum is one of the main *documenta* venues and the place where the first *documenta* was held in 1955.

What are your favourite *documenta* installations of all time?
I love *7000 Oaks* by Joseph Beuys from *documenta 7*. It's beautiful to see how it changed the city; wandering through Kassel, one can see his oaks everywhere. Another of my favourites is *The Vertical Earth Kilometer* by Walter de Maria, from *documenta 6*. The piece is a brass rod that extends one kilometre into the ground

on Friedrichsplatz. All that is visible of it is a two-inch-wide gold circle. It's a lesson in remembering to look below the surface.

Where else do you like to experience art in Kassel?
I'm always interested to see what is coming out of the city's art academy, Art University Kassel (Kunsthochschule Kassel). Some of the project spaces that have emerged from the art academy, such as Tokonoma and LAGE, have great programmes. I also like visiting the exhibitions at Kasseler Kunstverein and Neue Galerie, and the Gemäldegalerie Alte Meister at Schloss Wilhelmshöhe for classical art.

Is Kassel different from other cities known for art?
Because of *documenta*, the audience in Kassel is extremely open to and knowledgeable about contemporary art. At the Fridericianum, we've noticed that many people, both locals and international visitors, return to the same exhibition several times. That's quite exceptional.

How would you describe the people in Kassel?
From the moment I arrived in Kassel, I realised that people here are very open to new ideas.

Where is good in Kassel for a working lunch?
Ristorante Il Teatro, which serves very good Italian food, is very central and has a lovely atmosphere for a business lunch.

Which Kassel neighbourhood do you live in?
I've been living in the city centre since I moved to Kassel in 2013. Since I often work late, I wanted to be close to the Fridericianum; I live a three-minute walk away!

What is the best thing about living in Kassel?
Kassel is a great place for thinking. It's a small, calm city. After spending many years living in larger cities, I appreciate that about Kassel.

What do you find most visually striking in Kassel?
Kassel has become a city of migration; I think it's quite visible and beautiful.

Where do you go for inspiration?
The Karlsaue Park is stunning and huge, and it's a three-minute walk from my office. I also like spending time in north Kassel. You get a feeling of different cultures and I really like spending time there. It's a good place to sit and think. And if you like Turkish dishes I can warmly recommend Tat Urfa.

Where is good for coffee and cake?
Café Nenninger, across from the Fridericianum, is a more traditional café with delicious homemade cakes.

Where do you go for a meal out?

I really like Restaurant Eckstein. They serve traditional German food in a low-key and private environment.

Where do you recommend for a drink?

I like Lolitabar, which is quite lively, or the Weinberg Krug, near Art University Kassel. And above all, I always enjoy the opening parties at the Fridericianum!

Where do you go to enjoy music in Kassel?

The International Minimal Music Festival held in Kassel every year is quite extraordinary. I'd also recommend going to St. Martin's Church (Martinskirche) for music recitals on the largest classical organ in Europe, built by German-Norwegian artist Yngve Holen and the architect Ivar Heggheim. The organ is quite amazing because it looks like a traditional instrument, but there's a metre of hair falling down from it, which moves when the organ is played.

What does your perfect day off in Kassel look like?

Sleeping in, reading, or going to one of the art house cinemas such as Filmladen, Gloria, or Bali cinema.

How would you advise visitors to Kassel to get lost in the city and discover it for themselves?

Kassel is a micro cosmos. Compared to larger cities, everything in Kassel is more visible. Visitors should make the most of this by walking and making their own discoveries.

Find out more about Susanne Pfeffer at www.fridericianum.org

chapter 2

Work

*Find out the basics of working in Kassel,
co-working and networking.*

Photo: Minu Lee for Aust & Amelung

Creative and start-up hub

Kassel isn't the first city you'd think of to set up an entrepreneurial venture or to start a creative idea. Cast as the place the art world takes notice of once every five years at *documenta*, it's an oft-forgotten fact that the city exists for the remaining 1,725 non-*documenta* days of every five years too. It doesn't only exist, it thrives. While *documenta* and the Art University Kassel (Kunsthochshule Kassel) have inspired many creative and artistic ventures, Kassel has also become a centre of innovation and tech entrepreneurship, thanks in part to the Science Park.

Kassel is a small city, with lower rents and a greater abundance of space compared to elsewhere. Freelancers have more options for working locations than they do in cities where office rents are prohibitive, but Kassel locals see this as an additional, if attractive, bonus. Many successful Kassel start-up owners are often told they should move to a larger city to build on their success. They're continuously telling people: 'We're doing very well in Kassel, thank you very much!'

Lower rents mean the co-working trend isn't exactly booming in Kassel, as it is in larger neighbouring cities. Yet the concept of co-working is a perfect fit for the creative and entrepreneurial culture in Kassel, despite the fact there are currently only a few co-working spaces to choose from. The spaces that do exist are ideal for digital nomads and travelling entrepreneurs, with spacious interiors and flexible co-working options. The lack of co-working spaces may well change in years to come too, as the Economic Region of Kassel (Wirtschaftsförderung Region Kassel) has noticed a boom in demand for offices, with localised creative industries emerging and taking hold.

In the meantime, there's an abundance of opportunities to network and collaborate. There are Meetups and networking groups aplenty, while the city plays host to a year-round selection of events ideal for gaining inspiration and developing new contacts.

When it comes to working culture, a more current trend in Kassel is for a few freelancers to get together and hire an office space as a group. They do this so they don't have to work from home alone, but also so they can benefit from the social and networking opportunities that come with working around others.

Visitors to Kassel used to big city attitudes should remember that Kassel – as a smaller pond – makes people more approachable. If you're visiting Kassel and have found a local business you find inspiring and fits with your own line of work, make contact with the owners and arrange to meet up while you're in the city. This is how long-lasting connections in small cities such as Kassel are made, and it's a refreshing way to do business.

Work essentials

Find out a little more about some of the practicalities of working or setting up business in Kassel.

Bank accounts

Take your passport and visa, if applicable, to your bank of choice, along with your residency registration (Anmeldebestätigung) document if you're a non-EU national (obtained from an immigration office/ Ausländerbehorde). Banks in Kassel include:

Deutsche Bank
www.deutsche-bank.de
Kasseler Sparkasse
www.kasseler-sparkasse.de
Kasseler Bank
www.kasselerbank.de

Business registration

Before commencing business activity, notify the regulatory agency (Ordnungsamt) in your local Kassel district. This registration notifies the tax office, Employers' Liability Insurance Association (Berufsgenossenschaft) and Chamber of Industry and Commerce.
www.serviceportal-kassel.de

Directory enquiries

To find out a telephone number, call:
11833 for national enquiries;
11834 for international enquiries;
11837 for the above services in English.

Telephone book websites include:
Tele-auskunft
www.teleauskunft.de
Das Telefonbuch
www.dastelefonbuch.de
Yellow Pages
www.gelbeseiten.de

Finding a job

There are a number of job websites and recruitment agencies serving Kassel.

Kassel job sites include:
Jobs Kassel:
www.jobs-kassel.de
Meinestadt:
jobs.meinestadt.de
Stellenanzeigen:
www.stellenanzeigen.de

Health insurance

EU citizens who work for an employer pay 50% of health insurance costs; the employer pays the remaining 50%. Self-employed individuals must pay the full cost. The Artists Social Fund (Künstler Sozialkasse/KSK) is a subsidised programme to pay health and pension contributions for artists.
www.kuenstlersozialkasse.de

Learn German

It's wise to learn some German if you want to truly integrate in Kassel, especially if you want to do business. There are a number of language schools, some with business focused classes. Kassel language schools include:

Berlitz:
www.berlitz.de/kassel
Institut für Sprachen:
www.ifs-kassel.de
International Study Centre (ISC), University of Kassel:
www.uni-kassel.de/ einrichtungen/en/sprz/ sprachenzentrum

Residency registration

Anyone moving to Kassel needs to visit a local Residence Registration Office (Einwohnermeldeamt or Bürgeramt) to register their residency within two weeks of finding a residence (i.e. not a hotel or hostel). A passport, lease or rental agreement and a registration form are needed to do so. Registration results in an income tax card and an official registration document (Anmeldebestätigung), which is needed to gain access to other services, e.g. opening a bank account.
www.serviceportal-kassel.de

SIM cards

A number of pre-paid SIMs also give access to the internet for a fixed fee per month, which is approximately €10 per month for 500MB or €20 per month for 5GB. Kassel SIM providers include:
Aldi Talk:
www.alditalk.de
O2:
www.o2online.de
Vodafone:
www.vodafone.de

Tax

Business owners must file tax returns: monthly during the first year of operation, and annually thereafter. Corporation tax, trade tax and income tax must also be paid in advance once a quarter. Business owners should get a tax accountant or tax lawyer to ensure the proper procedures are met. Once a year, all employees and business owners must submit tax refund forms too.
finanzamt-kassel.hessen.de

Visas

EU citizens who wish to undertake paid or self-employed work in Germany do not need work permits or visas; residents of other countries need a visa. Visas can be acquired in German embassies and consulates around the world. Non-EU citizens who have only decided to try to stay in Kassel after arrival in Germany need to contact the immigration office (Ausländerbehörde).
www.auslaenderaemter.de

Useful websites

Kassel Chamber of Industry and Commerce (CIC)
www.ihk-kassel.de
Kassel Serviceportal
www.serviceportal-kassel.de
Stadt Kassel
www.stadt-kassel.de

Photo: Minu Lee for Aust & Amelung

Science Park Kassel

This start-up and innovation centre is comprised of more than 5,000m² of offices, laboratories and workshops. Found on the University of Kassel campus, this is a start-up hub of both spin-offs from the university and those who want to be close to the innovative university environment. Desks are also available in on-site co-working areas, on a daily or monthly basis. In addition co-workers have access to the Idea Lab for creative group work, a café lounge (The Science Lounge) and outdoor courtyard, as alternative spots to work and discuss ideas. Co-workers also have access to networking opportunities and events put on by the Science Park. Prices start from €15 per day (€9 for students) to €210 per month (€150 for students), with 24-hour access and an office address available for an extra cost.

Universitätsplatz 12, 34127
+49 (0)561 9537 9600
info@sciencepark-kassel.de
www.sciencepark-kassel.de
Tram: Mombachstrasse

More co-working locations

NDT Quality Center

This co-working space on the outskirts of Kassel is found inside the renovated admin building of an old concrete factory. The space makes nods to its more industrial past with some concrete features, but is also flooded with natural daylight. Co-workers have access to a pretty garden and terrace. Meeting and conference rooms are also available to hire. The co-working space is at the edge of the Dönche Nature Reserve (Naturschutzgebiet Dönche), a vast and rugged green space perfect for finding inspiration.
Korbacher Strasse 173, 34132
+ 49 (0)561 816 9340
info@ndtcenter.de
www.ndtcenter.de
Train: Kassel-Oberzwehren

Coworking Baunatal

Further out of the city centre, but still only a 20 minute drive or train journey from Kassel, is the functional Coworking Baunatal. Hourly, daily and monthly rates are available, and the space attracts an array of freelancers, start-up entrepreneurs and digital nomads.
An der Stadthalle 9, 34225
+49 (0)561 4739 6353
info@coworking-baunatal.de
www.coworking-baunatal.de
Train: Baunatal Stadtmitte

Work Oase Kassel

Also referred to as 'WOK', this functional co-working space squirrelled away down a private road, offers both flexible and fixed desks available to rent. As well as a desk, co-workers get access to the internet, printer, photocopier and fax. There's also the option of having an office address and post service. Prices start from €15 per day to €575 per quarter. Co-workers who have at least a week-long membership can gain 24 hour access to the space.
Fünffensterstrasse 2, 34117
+49 (0)561 989 54450
kontakt@workoasekassel.de
www.workoasekassel.de
Tram: Ständeplatz

See also

Immowelt:
www.immowelt.de/liste/kassel-mitte

Stephan Haberzettl

Filmmaker

Tell us about your work.
I'm a filmmaker and campaign creative. My film company, clipmedia, is an ideas agency for creative communication, and allows photography and film creatives to network. I spend most of my time working on political and cultural documentaries.

What is the creative working trend in Kassel?
It's a small city so there aren't large co-working spaces. Creatives don't like working at home alone either, so they rent offices together. The creative scene in Kassel is close-knit, so if you hear someone's ceiling is destroying his brain at home, they probably want to share an office space! Lots of Kassel's creatives work together on projects, so they rent a space like ours to work for a while. Sometimes it works so well, they keep on paying the rent.

Where do you work?
My office is called Marsanzüge (space suits). We like to think we're in the future and behind the moon, and it sounds similar to massanzüge (tailor-made suits), like the shops that were there before us. It's a tiny co-working shop in a 19th century house in Vorderer Westen, which we've furnished with a mixture of modern and vintage décor. I share the space with Jan Krögel, a graphic designer, but we have enough space to invite other creatives to come and work with us on joint projects. We constantly have interesting new people in our space. My office feels like a cuddly living room too; I love that homely feeling.

What's good about working in Kassel?
From Kassel I can travel to my customers in any major German city within three hours. As Kassel itself is quite small, you have easy access to other creatives and the great cultural scene.

Do you have any tips for creatives who want to come to Kassel to work?
Meet us for a tea at Marsanzüge! The best way to work here is to get to know other creatives.

Which project are you most proud of?
One of my most loved projects is artort.tv, which I established during *documenta* 11 in 2002. It's an art blog covering each *documenta* in film and photography.

What's your favourite thing to do in Kassel?
I love sitting in the Dönche Nature Reserve with a picnic and wine, enjoying nature and watching the sheep watching me.

Find out more about Stephan Haberzettl at www.clipmedia.de and www.artort.tv

Free Wi-Fi

If you enjoy the buzz of cafés or public spaces to do your work, you'll be pleased to know that free Wi-Fi can be found in plenty of locations across Kassel.

Here are our top tips for connecting to Wi-Fi for free:

Museums, galleries and Kassel hotspots

Kassel's well-known places have free Wi-Fi, so combining an inspiring visit with checking your emails is a possibility. Some of the most inspiring places to spend some time with a laptop include Café Jérôme by Schloss Wilhelmshöhe and the Orangerie in Karlsaue Park.
www.museum-kassel.de

Café Jérôme, Schlosspark 1, 34131
+49 (0)561 3109 7072
www.cafe-jerome.de
Tram: Wilhelmshöhe

Orangerie, Auedamm 20b, 34121
+49 (0)561 2861 0318
info@orangerie-kassel.de
www.orangerie-kassel.de
Tram: Friedrichsplatz

City centre

City-Point and Königs-Galerie, Kassel's two shopping centres, both have free Wi-Fi, and a choice of eateries to sit down in while you surf.

City-Point, Königsplatz 61, 34117
+49 (0)561 701 300
www.city-point-kassel.de
Tram: Königsplatz

Königs-Galerie, Neue Fahrt 12, 34117
+49 (0)561 700 080
info@koenigsgalerie.de
www.koenigsgalerie.de
Tram: Friedrichsplatz

Freifunk

This grassroots initiative is part of the international movement for a wireless community network. There are a number of connection points in Kassel.
www.freifunk-kassel.de

Instabridge or Wiffinity

These apps automatically connect you to Wi-Fi as soon as you're in range of participating providers. A handful of bars, cafés and public spaces provide free Wi-Fi in the Kassel area, meaning you can be online whenever you're in range.
www.instabridge.com
www.wiffinity.com

Netcom Kassel

This provider offers free Wi-Fi in central Kassel locations, including Königsplatz, Friedrichsplatz and Kassel Hauptbahnhof. Just search for 'NetcomCity Free'.
www.netcom-kassel.de

Rokkeberg Coffee & Juice

There are two branches of Rokkeberg in Kassel, and this city centre location is ideal for a laptop pit stop, particularly if you sit at one of the quieter tables upstairs. As well as free Wi-Fi, the coffee is top-notch and the décor has a touch of the Scandi-chic. It's also a concept store, so prepare to be tempted by a little retail therapy on your way out.
Ständeplatz 15, 34117
+49 (0)561 9868 0630
Facebook
@rokkebergcoffeeandjuice
Tram: Ständeplatz

Photo: Rokkeberg Coffee & Juice

Kazuo Katase

Artist

Kazuo Katase is a Japanese artist who has been living in Kassel since the 1970s. He has participated in the *documenta* exhibition, and has exhibited across the world, including in the National Museum of Modern Art and the Shoto Museum of Art in Tokyo, the Louisiana Museum of Modern Art in Denmark, the New Museum of Contemporary Art in New York, Staatsgalerie Stuttgart and Josef Albers Museum in Bottrop. Inspired by eastern and western philosophy, Katase works across many mediums, including stage design and architecture.

Introduce yourself.

I was born in Shizuoka, Japan. I thought I would be an artist from the age of 14, and I moved to Tokyo in 1967. It was always a metropolitan centre of Asia; an exciting and inspiring city with an active culture. After two solo exhibitions in 1973 and 1974 in galleries in Tokyo, I felt it was the logical time to move from the east to the west, for new experiences in western culture. I met the director of the Städtische Galerie Wolfsburg at around that time and in 1975, he invited me to undertake an artist residency there. Taking the step of leaving Japan was certainly an existential decision too. It was my choice and my desire to discover the strange and new experience of leaving my home country. It was my decision to be able to see myself more clearly in this way as well. After Wolfsburg, I moved to Kassel, a mid-size German city with an active source of contemporary art and home to the *documenta* exhibition. I studied experimental photography and free art, and pursued my artistic path.

What shapes your life philosophy?
Ontology and Zen Buddhism.

What influences your art?
Primarily, I'm inspired by philosophy and religion. The German philosopher
Martin Heidegger and the Japanese Zen Buddhist Daisetz T. Suzuki are two key
influences for me. I am a traveller, and on my journeys, my terrain is 'seeing'. It's
an unconditional seeing that seeks nothing and, precisely because of that, it can
allow ideas to appear. Everything I encounter is capable of being assimilated into
meaning. My images therefore lead directly back to the world.

Describe your contributions to the *documenta* exhibition.
At *documenta 9*, my installation *Nightmuseum* was exhibited in the Hall of the
Impressionists in the Neue Galerie. The installation worked with light and shadow,
the endangerment of art, human existence and multiple themes, viewed from
a pictorial perspective. This was the *documenta* exhibition curated by Jan Hoet,
the Belgian founder of the Municipal Museum for Contemporary Art (Stedelijk
Museum voor Actuele Kunst /SMAK). I met him in 1986, when I participated in
his *Guest Rooms* (*Chambres d'Amis*) exhibition, in Ghent, Belgium. In 1997, I was
invited by the Staatstheater Kassel to design the stage for *The Poor Heinrich* (*Die
Legende vom Armen Heinrich*), a piece by the playwright Tankred Dorst performed
for the *documenta 10* special programme.

What is Kassel like when *documenta* is happening?
Kassel becomes the heart of the art world for 100 days.

How do you describe your art?
In my artwork, I am always interested in space, objects and the intermediate realm
of things. To combine art, architecture, space and landscape to form a whole is a
fascinating challenge. I look back over my 50-year existence with contemporary
art, and I'm proud of what I have achieved as a freelance artist.

What is Kassel like from an artist's perspective?
For my work I need concentration, so having quiet space is crucial. As an artist, I
have discovered Kassel has just the right qualifications for working. This means
everything: if you can't work, how can you live? This is especially true in the
creative world. Of course, everyone has their own point of view and experience of
a place. This personal view is always connected with identity and existence.

Which Kassel neighbourhood do you live and work in?
Vorderer Westen, in the west of the city, the district characterised by the Founding
Epoch Architecture. Many of the flats in these old buildings have high ceilings
and that's what I like. My neighbours are normal locals of all generations and with
different professions. There are all kinds of little shops, and bio and conventional
supermarkets in the neighbourhood, as well as cafés, bistros and restaurants for
slow and fast food. But I don't see it as a question of whether I like it or not. It's a
question of existence.

Where can visitors to Kassel go to see your work?

The *Blue Dancer* spans over the Fulda river, and was first installed in 2003. It connects the oldest part of Kassel with the more newly-developed Unterneustadt, which had been totally ruined during World War II. My installation *Creation (Schöpfung)* is in the hospital called Diakonie Kliniken in Vorderer Westen. The atrium has a doorway to the patient garden and is open to the public.

What changes have you noticed in Kassel over the years?

Kassel's citizens, shops and restaurants have become much more multicultural and colourful compared to the 1970s. I really like this.

Why is Kassel a good place for creative people?

Creative people need to find a place and motivation. In Kassel, the locals are knowledgeable about contemporary art and there are opportunities to network. The living costs are still more moderate than in other metropolitan centres. This is an important point for creative people: having enough freedom as a freelancer. Kassel is convenient too. It's located in the middle of Germany and has a good train service to reach Frankfurt's airport and other centres across the country.

Where is your favourite place to work?

My artist studio – my 'dōjō' in Japanese – is always the best place. That's where I'm closest to myself.

What is the ideal way for you to take a break?

I like to sit at my table and drink a cup of green tea, which comes from my home prefecture in Japan.

Where are your favourite places for a meal out in Kassel?

There are many restaurants with international cuisine in Kassel, from nice bistros to local cafés, but I miss real Japanese restaurants. That's why it's really nice to have a Japanese dinner at home together with friends. For a casual lunch, I sometimes go to the Italian restaurant, Pizzeria Boccaccio, in Vorderer Westen. For a nice dinner, I like the Italian restaurant, Ristorante Il Teatro, or the Vietnamese restaurant, Da-Lat, which are both family-run businesses located in the centre of Kassel.

What do you like doing in your spare time?

Kassel has wonderful landscapes as its surroundings. I like to walk out in the open and in Kassel's beautiful parks, such as the UNESCO World Heritage landscape park, Bergpark Wilhelmshöhe, the Karlsaue Park, and along the Fulda river.

What is the current trend in Kassel?

The trend is for old, ragged districts in Kassel to become revived, such as the north of Kassel, including the Schillerviertel neighbourhood. There you find places such as the Werkstätten Brandthaus, which is a former clothing factory and now a centre for architecture students and creative people to do scale modelling.

There's also the up-and-coming new Fraunhofer IWES Institute for Energy System Technology.

<u>How should visitors to Kassel blend in and live like the locals do?</u>
There is a city cycling scheme, Konrad, which has cycle stations across Kassel. Visitors should hire bicycles or take the tram to discover the city and all her facets. Locals also pick up city magazines such as *FRIZZ* to find out what's going on.

<u>What does the future hold for Kassel?</u>
Artistic continuity and progress will carry on, alongside *documenta*, but also in its own right.

Find out more about Kazuo Katase at www.kazuo-katase.com

Working lunch

Whichever industry you work in, these spots are ideal for enjoying a business lunch.

La Vision
This cosy city centre restaurant is ideal for a tech-free (zero Wi-Fi!) business lunch. The family-run restaurant has been active in Kassel for decades, and the menu is full of hearty home-cooking with grilled meats and local flavours. It's a fabulous place to have a low fuss business lunch with a warm welcome.

Königs-Galerie, Neue Fahrt 12, 34117
+49 (0)561 207 9230
kovacs@lavision-kassel.de
www.lavision-kassel.de
Tram: Friedrichsplatz

Herkules Terrassen
If you have a little time and want inspiring surroundings, Herkules Terrassen in Bergpark Wilhelmshöhe is the place to go. Located in the famous UNESCO World Heritage mountain park, the views over both nature and the city are impressive. Sit inside or out, have a coffee and cake, or enjoy different menus for each part of the day. The restaurant-lounge is full of German specialities such as Flammkuchen and the Ahle Worscht, a sausage from the region, and hearty international flavours.

Schlosspark 26, 34131
+49 (0)561 - 9373 1910
info@herkules-terrassen.de
www.herkules-terrassen.de
Bus: Herkules

Falada

The restaurant and café of the Brothers Grimm Museum (GRIMMWELT) is a favourite among locals. The modern interior with a Scandi feeling makes way for the stunning views over lush greenery outside. The menu is 'soul food' with daily changing specialities, soups and salads. Food ranges from pumpkin and coconut soups, to red chicken curry or goulash. Falada is also a popular spot for an early evening drink or a mid-morning coffee and laptop session.

GRIMMWELT Kassel,
Weinbergstrasse 21, 34117
+49 (0)561 8104 5460
reservierung@faladakassel.de
www.faladakassel.de
Tram: Am Weinberg

© GRIMMWELT Kassel, Foto: Andreas Berthel

Networking

An array of networking events are on tap for Kassel's creative and tech community.

Science Park Kassel
This is Kassel's start-up and entrepreneurial hub, so it's also inevitably a great place for networking. Science Park Kassel has a vibrant calendar of events, which includes hearing from founders about their projects, *First Tuesday* workshops to upskill in different areas of business, and *fail nights*, popular in start-up circles to hear about business ideas that didn't work.
Universitätsplatz 12, 34127
+49 (0)561 9537 9600
info@sciencepark-kassel.de
www.sciencepark-kassel.de
Tram: Mombachstrasse

Tokonoma
This platform for art and subculture is a place to network with those involved in the arts and creative industries in Kassel. There's a weekly programme of lectures, screenings, talks, exhibitions, club nights and concerts – ideal for meeting like-minded people.
Frankfurterstrasse 58, 34121
info@supertokonoma.de
www.supertokonoma.de
Tram: Am Weinberg

flipdot
This much-loved hackerspace is a hub for coders, programmers and anyone remotely techie in the city. It's a place to be creative and learn about tech without the corporate culture. They host a variety of special events, from *pizza programming nights* to *eazy math* with beverages. Every Tuesday evening from 19:00, a hackerspace is open for anyone to attend.
Franz-Ulrich-Strasse 18, 34117
+49 (0)561 4739 5848
com@flipdot.org
www.flipdot.org
Train: Kassel Hauptbahnhof

Literaturhaus
This organisation supporting literature and the arts runs a range of events that are ideal for meeting like-minded people. They include salons with authors, open reading nights for people to present their own work, and visiting poets.
Kunsttempel, Friedrich-Ebert-Strasse 177, 34119
+49 (0)561 3169 0525
info@literaturhaus-nordhessen.de
www.literaturhaus-nordhessen.de
Tram: Kongress Palais / Stadthalle

Labor für Tisch- und Esskultur
This initiative by art students from Art School Kassel (Kunsthochschule Kassel) looks at how our relationship with food will change. It's ideal for food entrepreneurs to exchange ideas about food, the dining table and the cultures of eating. There are weekly events and kitchen workshops where experimentation is encouraged.
Facebook: Labor für Tisch- und Esskultur

Kassel Code Meetup
This is a popular Meetup for those active on Kassel's tech scene. Regular events mostly involve tech talks, where new software and hardware solutions are presented and discussed.
www.meetup.com/de-DE/KasselCodeMeetup

Caricatura
This vibrant museum runs a variety of events for anyone interested in the visual and graphical world. Events vary from readings and discussions about cartoons in film, to cartoon workshops on global issues. It's a breeding ground for ideas and discussion among everyone interested in the visual arts.
KulturBahnhof Kassel, Rainer-Dierichs-Platz 1, 34117
+49 (0)561 776 499
info@caricatura.de
www.caricatura.de
Train: Kassel Hauptbahnhof

Entrepreneurship Forum Nordhessen
This forum is for female entrepreneurs and self-employed businesswomen in the Nordhessen region. There are monthly meetings, lectures and workshops, open to anyone to attend without being a member.
+49 (0)560 491 8410
mail@unord.de
www.unord.de

Entrepreneurship & Startup Meetup Göttingen
This Meetup is in Göttingen, just 20 minutes away from Kassel by the ICE rail service. This Meetup is all about bringing together passionate entrepreneurs, founders, freelancers and people who are interested in entrepreneurship. It's a friendly community with plenty of ideas, with people keen on exchanging opinions, learning from experience, and connecting inspiring people.
www.meetup.com/Entrepreneurship-Startup-Meetup

Khesrau and Sohrab Noorzaie

Start-up entrepreneurs

Born in Afghanistan and raised in Kassel, Khesrau and Sohrab Noorzaie have used their university degrees and natural flair for entrepreneurialism to develop their start-up. SMINNO creates eco-friendly accessories manufactured in Germany to improve the functionality of everyday items. Their product line CESA started with the CESAtube amplifier for smartphones, followed by the CESAcruise hands-free kit for cyclists. Khesrau and Sohrab are well-known figures on Kassel's start-up scene and have won awards for their innovation.

Describe your background.

Khesrau: Our family came to Kassel from Afghanistan when we were children. Sohrab and I started working for ourselves in our twenties; our first business was an Italian restaurant, which we ran for 10 years. We also ran a promotions company while studying engineering and economics at the University of Kassel.

Sohrab: At some point, we wanted to create our own products, so we sold our businesses to focus on these. Although we had big and complex ideas, we recognised we needed to start small.

How did you come up with your business idea?

Sohrab: When we were on holiday! We wanted to listen to our music loudly, but we couldn't without speakers or amplifiers. We envisaged a zero-energy amplifier that suited all smartphones. We developed prototypes which worked really well, and CESAtube was born.

Khesrau: We also wanted to address the fact we couldn't find a satisfactory mount system for our bicycles. We imagined a secure hands-free kit which allowed us to take calls without wind noise and listen to music. So our second product was born, CESAcruise.

What is your philosophy on business and life?

Sohrab: We produce smart products that give customers more functionality and the feeling of independence. That's why we named our business SMINNO, which stands for SMart INNOvation. Our products are sustainable, universal, German-made and use high quality raw materials.

Khesrau: With every business we started, people told us it wasn't possible to be successful. This gave us energy. When people tell you that you can't do something, and then you do it... that's a feeling you can't buy. When you really want something, you can achieve it. That's our life philosophy.

Why is it important to develop German-made and sustainable products?

Khesrau: Production isn't only about profit. It's important that people think about where products come from and how their purchases affect the world. German-made products support the regional economy, and Germany still has the quality standards everyone knows and admires too. Short production and delivery processes and re-usable materials help minimise our ecological footprint.

What trends are your products responding to?

Sohrab: Customers want to use products for longer. Smartphones and accessories have a life of as little as six months before newer products come out. People are becoming more aware of the issues of sustainability, as well as their dependence on smartphone-specific products, and they don't necessarily like this constant manufacturing cycle.

What does the future hold for SMINNO?

Sohrab: Start-up life is really fast and comes with a lot of to-dos which have to be managed with little manpower. Step-by-step we're trying to have more structure in our business, to move from being a start-up to a well-established company.

Khesrau: We're working on new products that will be world firsts, so we need a bigger team to help us. We'll also be growing the European market beyond Germany and Spain to the Netherlands, France and Denmark. And after that, we want the world!

What is your proudest achievement?

Khesrau: Every year, the Hessen region has a *Hessen Champions* awards ceremony, a bit like the Oscars for companies. In 2016 we won the innovation category. Coming from Afghanistan 23 years earlier, to becoming recognised business owners, was personally very momentous. We're proud to go down in the history books of Hessen.

Sohrab: We were up against big companies with a lot of sales, technologies and innovative products. The innovation award recognises we're doing something in a new way. It's an honour.

Why is Kassel is a good place to have a business?

Khesrau: Kassel is a growing city with an expanding start-up community. For us, this combines well with having our family, friends and favourite hotspots nearby. We feel positive, motivated and focused here. Being in the middle of Germany is convenient too.

Sohrab: Kassel offers a great work-life balance and ranks highly as a place to live, work or be a student. It's really good more people are realising Kassel's potential.

Tell us about the Science Park, Kassel's start-up hub.

Sohrab: The University of Kassel has become a centre for the city's growing start-up scene and the Science Park was built as a home for this. We were invited to be one of the first Science Park companies. There's a great community and it allows us to work closely with the university.

Khesrau: The Science Lounge on-site is a great place to go for business meetings; all the start-ups go there for lunch or coffee.

Tell us about your life in Kassel.

Sohrab: Kassel's a small, multicultural city and we have always lived and worked near north Kassel. Khesrau and I live together, work together, play sport together and have the same friends! Our parents always taught us to be a team; it helps there's only one year age difference between us.

Khesrau: In a smaller city, you can't go undercover! As we're in business and have been in the newspaper, we're regularly recognised. We're happy when people say: 'Nice work, guys.' It's better than getting lost in a big city where nobody recognises what you're doing.

Describe the north Kassel neighbourhood.

Sohrab: It's changed a lot in the last few years, becoming an area full of arts and culture. It's increasingly popular, and people say they want to be part of the alternative crowd who live here. The outsides of the houses don't look that good, but if you go inside, you're impressed.

What other Kassel neighbourhoods do you like?

Sohrab: Wilhelmshöhe is a relaxing area for walking and visiting the Schloss Wilhelmshöhe palace and the Hercules statue, which is famous in Kassel. The surrounding area is known for its curative mineral springs and spas; we like Kurhessen Therme. Brasselsberg is a very classy neighbourhood too.

Khesrau: The centre is good for shopping and meeting friends. Bigger cities are made up of several centres, but here everything is nearby. Kassel is well-known for all its green spaces. Karlsaue Park is a great place for a run, or to chill out with friends. The Auestadion is nearby which is packed every time there's a sporting event.

Where do you go for coffee?

Sohrab: Cafeteria Pavillon, in the university, is a place we belong. When we were developing our business idea, it's the place we would go to discuss it. We still go for a coffee there most days. It's a place to be immersed in the student life of Kassel, and the coffee is cheap!

Khesrau: We always stop for a coffee at ALEX too. You can sit outside and it's a cool place to be surrounded by city life.

Where do you like to eat out in Kassel?
Khesrau: Avanti is an Italian restaurant in the city centre we go to often. Restaurant Lehmofen and Café Hurricane are some of the really good Turkish restaurants in the city.
Sohrab: Falafel Grillpoint is a place we enjoy every time, where you can eat Arabic and Lebanese food. Take Hallali Burger is another of our favourites; they serve the best burgers in town.

Where is good for a drink?
Khesrau: Cafe Bohemia is part of Kassel's history now: it's been there for 30 years and it's great for a drink, coffee or to smoke. It's on Friedrich-Ebert-Strasse, which is full of people during the weekends and summertime.
Sohrab: We also like King Schulz Bar. And Casa Colombiana runs an after-work party every three months. A lot of business people go there, so it's a go-to event if you want to know who is doing what.

How does Kassel feel when the *documenta* exhibition is on?
Khesrau: Kassel feels alive during *documenta*. Everyone is talking about new things and there are so many people coming and going, speaking different languages. It makes Kassel feel big and important.

Where do you go to get away from it all?
Sohrab: The Orangerie coffee bar in Karlsaue Park is a place we can take a few minutes for ourselves and talk about things other than business. During the summer, we cycle there after work.

What is the quintessential image of Kassel?
Sohrab: When you're driving into Kassel on the Kasseler Berge highway from the north, there's a spot where you see the whole city panorama in front of you. I've worked in a lot of cities in the past, but I've never found a view like that.

What music is on your Kassel soundtrack?
Sohrab: Kassel is an open place where you find mixtures of everything. I think the guys from *Milky Chance*, who come from Kassel, really capture that. It's upbeat music that's not just one genre: perfect for Kassel.

What is your advice to other aspiring entrepreneurs?
Khesrau: Do it! In entrepreneurial work, most people say your idea won't work, and only a few say it will. Don't be afraid. You can see along the way if it works, and if it doesn't, modify your approach. It's important to start something; everything else will come from that.

Read more about SMINNO at www.sminno.de or on Facebook @sminno.de

chapter 3

Live

*Retailers, bars and eateries with flair,
a haven for creatives and some
nice pillows to put your head on.*

Live in Kassel

Kasselaners revel in the city's many creative corners for eating, drinking and general meandering. The culturally-rich mood heightens during the *documenta* exhibition, but visitors will be surprised at the visionary amenities the locals have on their doorsteps, whatever the time of year. Combining traditional German with a touch of cutting-edge creative, hotels, shops, eateries and drinking holes offer exhilarating fusions of style.

The locals love coffee and there's no shortage of options in the city, from cafés with on-site micro-roasteries to avant-garde concept stores providing total immersion in coffee, shopping and art. Eating out in Kassel ranges from Michelin-starred quality to the low-key Turkish eateries serving mouth-watering cuisine. Peppered with traditional German and eclectic international restaurants, there's something for everyone. There's no shortage of bars and beer gardens either, serving everything from locally brewed honey beers to inventive cocktails.

Shopping in Kassel is an innovative experience too. While the centre is full of high street shops, taking just a few steps off the beaten track uncovers tiny boutiques with true flair, selling everything from handmade illustrated books and upcycled fashion, to carefully curated antiques. Friedrich-Ebert-Strasse in particular has become a haven for craftsmanship and socialising, having won several awards in recent years.

When Kassel locals aren't enjoying all of this, they're making the most of the rest of what Kassel has to offer. With green spaces in abundance, clearing the mind with a walk in a park or along the river is a common pastime. Kassel's galleries, cultural institutions and a handful of museums complete the picture of a small city that packs the punch of a larger one.

This chapter is all about eating, drinking, shopping, sleeping and generally living in Kassel. All of the recommendations you find here come from our Kassel interviewees and other locals who live in the city. We've also included a few recommendations of the most entrepreneurial and creative innovations going on in Kassel, giving you a flavour of some of the most inventive things going on in the city.

Photos: pentahotels

pentahotel Kassel

This design hotel in the Wilhelmshöhe district of Kassel is found between the city centre and the famous Bergpark. Super-convenient for those arriving by long distance train, pentahotel Kassel is a tasteful retreat from the rest of the world. The hotel's design credentials are masterminded by the award-winning Matheo Thun, who has worked with Porsche Design, Missoni, Lavazza and Bulgari. The hotel is all exposed brick walls and astutely-lit glass, faux animal print armchairs and virtual fireplaces. Rooms have a laid-back design and all the mod-cons, including rain showers and iPod connectors. Communal areas include a gym and sauna, games room and the pentalounge, ideal for food, drink and chilling.

Bertha-von-Suttner-Strasse 15, 34131
+49 (0)561 933 9887
info.kassel@pentahotels.com
www.pentahotels.com/kassel
Train/tram: Kassel-Wilhelmshöhe

Foto-Motel

This eccentric guest house on the site of a former brothel is full of bright, chintzy furniture and a homely vibe. No two rooms are the same but all are as quirky as the owners, with modern paintings, tiled murals and plenty of antique bric-a-brac. Guests who come to stay, from tradesmen to university professors, are attracted by all things unconventional. Rooms are available as en-suites or with shared bathrooms; there are a couple of apartments with kitchen facilities too. All guests have access to a courtyard garden with chairs, tables and plants growing out of every nook and cranny. There's also a complimentary breakfast, a library, plenty of artistic installations and the odd impromptu music concert. The hotel's big sister, Festerzumhof, is just around the corner, on the former site of a factory that used to manufacture antennae.

Wolfhager Strasse 53, 34117
+49 (0)561 861 6820
knocking@foto-motel.de
www.foto-motel.de
Tram: Lutherplatz

Photos: Foto-Motel

43

Other hotels

Hotel Schweizer Hof
This modern hotel has suites and one or two bedroom apartments with kitchenettes. There are special rates for those staying for 30 days or longer. The hotel design is contemporary and comfortable, and rooms are ideal for digital nomads, with laptop-sized safes and iPhone/iPod docking stations. There's also a free breakfast buffet, a spa with a Finnish sauna and a pendant lit lobby bar.

Wilhelmshöher Allee 288, 34131
+49 (0)561 93 690
info@hotel-schweizerhof-kassel.de
www.hotel-schweizerhof-kassel.de
Tram: Kunoldstrasse

TRYP by Wyndham
Art Nouveau lovers feel right at home in this city centre hotel: the first steel and concrete structure in the city, built 100 years ago. The plush lobby is filled with rich wooden décor and leather couches, while the pièce de résistance is a domed glass ceiling flooding natural light inside. Rooms are spacious and comfortable, with elegant desks ideal for working, while evenings are spent in the communal games room playing or watching billiards.

Erzbergerstrasse 1-5, 34117
+49 (0)30 9780 8888
info@trypkassel.com
www.trypkassel.com
Train: Kassel Hauptbahnhof

Renthof Kassel
One of the newest hotels in Kassel is found in a faithfully restored historic building dating back to 1298. Throughout the ages, the building has been a monastery, a knight academy, a university and a courthouse. Now a design hotel, there are 55 individually designed suites, a library, bar, restaurant and a moodily-lit courtyard. There's even a church that can be used as an event space.

Baunsbergstrasse 60, 34131
+49 (0)561 2078 8125
info@renthof-kassel.de
www.renthof-kassel.de
Bus: Freibad Wilhelmshöhe

Photo: Renthof Kassel

Oliver Stokowski

Actor

This renowned actor has appeared in dozens of films, television series and productions in the world's most famous theatres. Among many others, his filmography credits include *The Book Thief*, *The Experiment* and *Regular Guys*, while his TV credits include *Crossing Lines* and *Midlife Crisis*. Born and raised in Kassel, Oliver still considers the city to be home, despite having travelled the globe for his work.

Introduce yourself.

I'm married to an actress and I'm the proud father of two sons; one's a teenager and the other is a baby. I was born in Kassel in the 1960s. My father was a police Chief Inspector, and my mother was a housewife. My great-grandfather was the famous conductor Leopold Stokowski, who was known for conducting music in esteemed orchestras across the world. He also conducted the music for several Hollywood films, including Disney's *Fantasia*.

What is memorable about your childhood in Kassel?

I learned to walk in the Fuldaaue and the beautiful Bergpark Wilhelmshöhe. During my childhood, there were fabulous toboggan runs winding their way through the huge forests in Brasselsberg in the midst of the mountainous Kasseler Berge. There were small ski-lifts too, so this is where I learned to ski as a young boy.

How did you get into acting?

My career started at the Staatstheater Kassel, where I took my first steps on stage as a teenager. There was an advert in the newspaper saying they were looking for 'strong young men' as extras. At that time I was a very slim guy with long blond hair. So I put on three pullovers and two pairs of trousers and went for the casting. I got the role!

What happened next?

My real artistic exploration happened while acting at school. My teachers told me I belonged on stage. Nevertheless, I decided to pursue musical studies, playing the piano and double bass, at the University of Kassel. I also played in a youth orchestra and in several bands. I financed my studies – and my first car, a VW Beetle – by playing jazz sessions in Kassel and surrounding cities. After a while – and after completing my alternative social service as a paramedic in Kassel – I went to study acting at the University of Music and Performing Arts in Graz, Austria, which was recommended to me by an actress friend. This was the beginning of the 1980s. Kassel had already become *documenta*-Stadt and gained worldwide fame. It encouraged me to pursue my dreams.

Where has your career taken you since?

After my studies, I played in many renowned theatres, including Munich, Zurich, Vienna, Hamburg and Paris. I appeared in guest performances everywhere from China to Riga. In parallel, I have always worked in the movies and TV, from playing the criminal inspector in the famous series *The Investigator (Der Ermittler)* to international productions such as *Crossing Lines*. So far, I have had the pleasure of working with some notable directors including Thomas Vinterberg, Alvis Hermanis, Oliver Hirschbiegel, Brian Percival and Matthias Hartmann. I'm currently playing at the Deutsches Theater in Berlin and the Burgtheater in Vienna. I'm also preparing for a new production in Vienna and the summertime Salzburger Festspiele. Additionally, I'm preparing for a TV-movie and I'm on the promotional tour for the motion picture, *Short Term Memory Loss*, by Andreas Arnstedt, where I play the leading role of a former boxer who has lost his memory.

Which Kassel neighbourhood feels like home?

When I'm in Kassel, which is every couple of months, I visit my parents or my uncle in Goethestrasse, Vorderer Westen. It's a very trendy area now, with many cafés, bars and little shops. You see hipsters and young families like you do in Prenzlauer Berg or Mitte in Berlin. Across the street there are two parks, Aschrottpark and Goetheanlage, where my uncle and I love to go for walks with his many dogs.

Where do you find inspiration in Kassel?

For me, Kassel is the perfect city for walking; you can reach almost everywhere by foot or bicycle. I love to learn my lines while strolling in the Bergpark Wilhelmshöhe.

What is a favourite pastime of Kassel locals?

The first Saturday of every month from June to September, there is a great spectacle involving the illuminated water features at nightfall in Bergpark Wilhelmshöhe. It's accompanied by the *Wassermusik* of Georg Friedrich Händel and hundreds of burning torches. Sometimes, by chance, a little mist comes over, and you find yourself in a Brothers-Grimm-inspired magical fairy tale setting. It may sound like a tourist attraction, but it's the locals who make the most of it. They come along with blankets, parasols and picnics. They also do this during the Water Games (Wasserspiele) every summer, where visitors can follow the whole course of the water through the park.

What would your ideal weekend in Kassel involve?

I like to visit the Gemäldegalerie Alte Meister in Schloss Wilhelmshöhe, where you can enjoy the old masters in felt slippers. The Glass House (Gewächshaus) in Bergpark Wilhelmshöhe is beautiful and inspiring. It's a greenhouse with orchids, camellias, banana plants and hundreds of other deliciously smelling flowers and plants. The intense smell of an ocean of flowers is a smell I connect with Kassel. I also enjoy walking through the busy Königsstrasse, passing the redesigned Königsplatz. I love the Fridericianum, then stopping in the Orangerie for a coffee. The terrace there is a real highlight, and is part of the *Laserscape* installation by Horst H. Baumann and Peter Hertha from *documenta 6*: the first permanent laser sculpture in the world.

Where's the best place in Kassel to get away from it all?

The Karlsaue Park and the Fuldaaue. I walk for hours, recharging with new energy by inhaling the beautiful landscape.

Is there anything you enjoy in Kassel now you're a father?

I often take my older son to the marvellous Natural History Museum (Naturkundemuseum) in the Ottoneum. It's been redesigned many times and every time we visit, we're inspired and enthusiastic about the great exhibitions.

What signifies a quintessential Kassel summertime?

The Bugasee is a lake in the Fuldaaue which was made for the National Garden Show (Bundesgartenschau); nowadays it's nice for swimming in the summer. Afterwards, it's perfect to lie on the grass with a smoothie bought from a food truck.

What's your top tip for culture in Kassel?

Don't miss the Staatstheater Kassel, a triple genre theatre and a prestigious venue for drama, opera and dance.

Where do you like to go for coffee?

At the Rokkeberg concept store on Goethestrasse you can do some cool shopping for clothes and furniture while drinking coffee. I also love to sit on the terrace of the Kollektivcafé Kurbad, whether it's to have a coffee and one of their fine cakes in the afternoon, or a glass of wine at sunset while overlooking the Fulda river. The café is run by five young guys and it's a venue for cultural events, music, literature, and political life. It's the perfect place for me to work on my laptop, making notes for my roles.

Where do you like to eat out in Kassel?

I like denkMAHL on Friedrich-Ebert-Strasse for breakfast, lunch, dinner or the beer garden. I love Italian food too, for which I'd recommend the classy and cosy Il Teatro.

Where's good for a drink and an evening out?

Vinobar Il Teatro, next to the restaurant, is an excellent wine bar. Bar Seibert is a rather chic place for good cocktails. My niece likes King Schulz Bar, which is a very cool bar with vintage design and references to the hipster styles of Berlin. Another monthly highlight is the poetry slam by Felix Römer in the Panoptikum club.

Describe Kassel during *documenta*.

documenta is the greatest highlight of Kassel. It's a huge source of inspiration for all creatives coming to and living in Kassel. As an actor, it gives me a lot of inspiration for my roles. People from across the world come to our tiny city, spreading their stories and emotions, ideas and ideals. That creates a special feeling. I remember the *7000 Oaks* by Joseph Beuys, a landscape artwork he started in 1982 at *documenta 7* and finished at *documenta 8*, with the help of many volunteers. There was an incredible energy flowing through Kassel. Beuys, the provocant who combined politics and art so intensely, gave Kassel so much. I admire him deeply.

How would you sum up Kassel?

Kassel is alive and simmering with creativity, yet it's relaxed. It's not as self-exposing as Berlin can sometimes be. The people of Kassel are laidback and love their city for what it is; no more, no less. During *documenta*, everybody goes to the exhibitions: grandmothers and teenagers, families and students, workers and managers. They are all curious to see what this marvellous event makes of their city this time around. And what Kassel makes of *documenta* this time around too. I experience Kassel as a young city, particularly as it has so many students now. It's always changing and in motion. But it's a smooth, floating motion, not a pushy one.

Find out more about Oliver Stokowski at www.imdb.com

Eating

Abessina
Ethiopian
Kurt-Schumacher-Strasse 23, 34117
+49 (0)561 5039 9263
abessina-restaurant-kassel.com
Tram: Am Stern
Carmen likes this place

Ahlemächt'jer
Burgers
Wildemannsgasse 1, 34117
+49 (0)173 611 3601
info@ahlemächtjer.de
www.ahlemächtjer.de
Tram: Altmarkt/
Regierungspräsidium
Kira and Sophie like this place

Avanti
Italian
Königs-Galerie, Obere
Königsstrasse 39, 34117
+49 (0)561 719 601
info@avanti.koenigsgalerie.de
Facebook @Avanti.Kassel
Tram: Friedrichsplatz
Khesrau and Sohrab like this place

Bashis Delight
Indian Ayurvedic slow food
Elfbuchenstrasse 18, 34119
+49 (0)561 739 7667
post@bashi.de
www.bashi.de
Tram: Friedenskirche
Kira and Sophie like this place

Café Bistro Hurricane
Turkish
Gottschalkstrasse 38, 34127
+49 (0)561 898 072
kontakt@hurricane-kassel.de
www.hurricane-kassel.de
Tram: Mombachstrasse
Khesrau and Sohrab like this place

Da-Lat
Vietnamese
Weisser Hof 1, 34117
+49 (0)561 17 074
Tram: Altmarkt/
Regierungspräsidium
Kazuo likes this place

denkMAHL
German
Friedrich-Ebert-Strasse 98, 34119
+49 (0)561 12 215
mail@denkmahl.com
www.denkmahl.com
Tram: Querallee
Oliver likes this place

El Erni
Spanish
Parkstrasse 42, 34119
+49 (0)561 710 018
www.el-erni.de
Tram: Querallee
Carl likes this place

Falafel Grillpoint
Middle Eastern
Werner-Hilpert-Strasse 20, 34117
+49 (0)157 3774 0622
Facebook @falafel.grill.point.kassel
Train: Kassel Hauptbahnhof
Khesrau and Sohrab like this place

Gambero Rosso
Italian
Gräfestrasse 4, 34121
+49 (0)561 285 381
gamberorosso@arcor.de
www.gamberorosso-kassel.de
Tram: Kirchweg
Carl likes this place

Hans Wurst
German sausages
Wolfhager Strasse 179, 34127
+49 (0)561 861 7383
Train: Kassel Hauptbahnhof
Carl likes this place

Heimat
German
Friedrich-Ebert-Strasse 118, 34119
+49 (0)561 8165 9224
kontakt@heimat-kassel.de
www.heimat-kassel.de
Tram: Friedenskirche
Carl likes this place

Humboldt 1a
Modern European
Humboldtstrasse 1a, 34117
+49 (0)561 7664 9755
info@humboldt1a.de
www.humboldt1a.de
Tram: Rathaus
Carl likes this place

Kleine Kantine
Seasonal European
Wildemannsgasse 1, 34117
+49 (0)561 734 0455
kontakt@kleinekantine.de
www.kleinekantine.de
Tram: Altmarkt/
Regierungspräsidium
Kira and Sophie like this place

Markthalle Kassel
Food stands
Wildemannsgasse 1, 34117
+49 (0)561 780 395
www.markthalle-kassel.de
Tram: Altmarkt
Carl likes this place

NACHBAR
Burgers
Frankfurter Strasse 76, 34121
+49 (0)176 9858 3968
nachbarkassel@gmail.com
Tram: Am Weinberg
Carmen likes this place

Namaste
Indian
Treppenstrasse 9, 34117
+49 (0)561 2026 0398
Tram: Scheidemannplatz
Carl likes this place

Pho Vang
Vietnamese
Garde-du-Corps-Strasse 1, 34117
+49 (0)561 937 1536
www.pho-vang.de
Tram: Rathaus
Carmen, Kira and Sophie like this place

Pizzeria Boccaccio
Italian
Querallee 36, 34119
+49 (0)561 4302 0410
www.boccaccio-kassel.de
Tram: Querallee
Kazuo likes this place

Restaurant Eckstein
German
Obere Königsstrasse 4, 34117
+49 (0)561 713 300
www.eckstein-kassel.de
Tram: Rathaus
Susanne likes this place

Restaurant Ilyssia
Greek
Lange Strasse 83, 34131
+49 (0)561 311 793
info@ilyssia.de
www.ilyssia.de
Tram: Hessischer Rundfunk
Carl likes this place

Restaurant Lehmofen
Turkish
Magazinstrasse 19, 34125
+49 (0)561 8706 6762
www.bistro-lehmofen.de
Tram: Weserspitze
Khesrau and Sohrab like this place

Ristorante Il Teatro
Italian
Oberste Gasse 9, 34117
+49 (0)561 287 2675
kontakt@ilteatro-kassel.de
www.ilteatro-kassel.de
Tram: Königsplatz
Kazuo, Oliver and Susanne like this place

Sapori D'Italia
Italian
Dörnberg Strasse 1, 34119
+49 (0)561 474 9524
info@sapori-kassel.de
www.sapori-kassel.de
Tram: Bebelplatz
Kira and Sophie like this place

Shinyu Sushi House
Japanese
Friedrich-Ebert-Strasse 79, 34119
+49 (0)561 739 7718
www.shinyu.de
Tram: Queralle
Kira and Sophie like this place

Stulle & Gut
Fusion events
post@stulleundgut.de
Facebook @stulleundgut
Carmen likes this place

Sushi Bar
Japanese
Schönfelder Strasse 38, 34121
+49 (0)561 9532 5757
www.sushibarkassel.de
Tram: Kirchweg
Carmen likes this place

Take Hallali Burger
Burgers
Theaterstrasse 1, 34117
+49 (0)561 7669 7000
Facebook @takehallaliburger
Tram: Friedrichsplatz
Khesrau and Sohrab like this place

Tat Urfa
Turkish
Untere Königsstrasse 89, 34117
+49 (0)561 984 4639
www.tat-urfa.de
Tram: Am Stern
Susanne likes this place

Voit
Modern international
Friedrich-Ebert-Strasse 86, 34119
+49 (0)561 5037 6612
post@voit-restaurant.de
www.voit-restaurant.de
Tram: Queralle
Carl likes this place

Weissenstein
Regional organic
Königstor 46, 34117
+49 (0)561 8409 5519
www.weissenstein-kassel.de
Tram: Karthäuserstrasse
Carl likes this place

Coffee

ALEX
Obere Königsstrasse 28a, 34117
+49 (0)561 766 170
hallo@dein-alex.de
www.dein-alex.de/kassel
Tram: Friedrichsplatz
Khesrau and Sohrab like this place

Café Buch-Oase
Germaniastrasse 14, 34119
+49 (0)176 2272 6511
mail@cafebuchoase.de
www.cafebuchoase.de
Tram: Kirchweg
Carmen likes this place

Café DesAStA
Arnold Bode Strasse 6, 34127
Facebook
@KaffeTrinkenImDesasta
Tram: Holländischer Platz/
Universität
Carmen likes this place

Café Nenninger
Friedrichsplatz 8, 34117
+49 (0)561 766 1690
kontakt@cafe-nenninger.de
www.cafe-nenninger.de
Tram: Friedrichsplatz
Susanne likes this place

Cafeteria Pavillon
University of Kassel, Diagonale
13, 34127
+49 (0)561 804 2444
www.studentenwerk-kassel.de
Tram: Mombachstrasse
Khesrau and Sohrab like this place

Kafe NEU Am Weinberg
Frankfurterstrasse 54, 34121
+49 (0)561 8164 8366
kassel@weinbergkrug.com
www.weinberg-kafe.de
www.weinbergkrug.de
Tram: Am Weinberg
Carmen likes this place

Kollektivcafé Kurbad
Sternstrasse 22, 34123
+49 (0)157 3208 4420
cafekollektivkassel@gmail.com
www.kollektivcafe-kurbad.org
Tram: Altmarkt
Carmen and Oliver like this place

Melchior Coffee
Neue Fahrt 15, 34117
+49 (0)561 8164 1886
www.melchiorkassel.de
Tram: Friedrichsplatz
Kira and Sophie like this place

Papiercafé
Kunsthochschule Kassel,
Menzelstrasse 13-15, 34121
+49 (0)152 5953 3232
papiercafekassel@gmail.com
papiercafe.tumblr.com
Tram: Heinrich-Heine-Strasse/
Universität
Carmen likes this place

Rokkeberg
Goethestrasse 67, 34119
+49 (0)561 5035 7817
nico.di-carlo@rokkeberg.com
www.rokkeberg.com
Tram: Bebelplatz
Kira, Sophie and Oliver like this place

Seegert Kaffeerösterei
Friedrich-Ebert-Strasse 64, 34119
+49 (0)561 9528 1268
info@seegertkaffee.de
www.seegertkaffee.de
Tram: Querallee
Carl likes this place

The Orangerie
Auedamm 20b, 34121
+49 (0)561 2861 0318
info@orangerie-kassel.de
www.orangerie-kassel.de
Tram: Friedrichsplatz
Khesrau, Sohrab and Oliver like this place

The Science Lounge
Science Park, Universitätsplatz 12, 34127
+49 (0)561 9537 9600
info@sciencepark-kassel.de
www.sciencepark-kassel.de
Tram: Mombachstrasse
Khesrau and Sohrab like this place

WESTEND Café
Elfbuchenstrasse 18, 34119
+49 (0)561 920 1122
Facebook: WESTEND Café
Tram: Friedenskirche
Carl likes this place

Drinking

Bar Seibert
Friedrich-Ebert-Strasse 47, 34117
+49 (0)561 6902 2715
info@barseibert.de
www.barseibert.de
Tram: Karthäuserstrasse
Oliver likes this place

Brauhaus Zum Rammelsberg
Rammelsbergstrasse 4, 34131
+49 (0)561 316 2730
www.zum-rammelsberg.de
Tram: Kunoldstrasse
Carl likes this place

Cafe Bohemia
Friedrich-Ebert-Strasse 60, 34119
+49 (0)561 16 391
www.bohemia-kassel.de
Tram: Annastrasse
Khesrau and Sohrab like this place

Caricatura Bar
Rainer-Dierichs-Platz 1, 34117
+49 (0)561 739 4206
wibkeroeder@caricatura.de
www.caricatura-bar.de
Train: Hauptbahnhof
Kira and Sophie like this place

Casa Colombiana
Friedrichstrasse 36, 34117
+49 (0)561 109 4930
Facebook @Casa.colombiana
Tram: Rathaus
Khesrau and Sohrab like this place

Chacal
Goethestrasse 44, 34119
+49 (0)561 777 444
Tram: Goethestrasse
Carmen likes this place

Fes Musikbar
Karthäuserstrasse 17, 34117
+49 (0)561 773 411
www.luunaa.de/fes-kassel
Tram: Karthäuserstrasse
Kira and Sophie like this place

King Schulz Bar
Weigelstrasse 14, 34117
+49 (0)561 5034 7565
info@kingschulz.de
www.kingschulz.de
Tram: Karthäuserstrasse
Khesrau, Sohrab, Kira, Sophie and Oliver like this place

Lolitabar
Part of Club A.R.M.
Werner-Hilpert-Strasse 22, 34117
+49 (0)561 713 147
www.armaberokay.de
Train: Kassel Hauptbahnhof
Susanne likes this place

Mutter
Bunsenstrasse 15, 34127
+49 (0)561 894 278
Facebook @MutterBar
Tram: Mombachstrasse
Carl likes this place

Panoptikum
Club with monthly poetry slam
Leipziger Strasse 407, 34123
+49 (0)178 862 3569
Facebook @panoptikum.kassel
Tram: Am Kupferhammer
Oliver likes this place

Rondell
Renthof, 35117
+49 (0)152 2958 1684
www.rondell-kassel.de
Tram: Altmarkt
Carmen likes this place

Steckenpferd
Kastenalsgasse 8, 34117
info@braumanufaktur-steckenpferd.de
braumanufaktur-steckenpferd.de
Tram: Altmarkt/Regierungspräsidium
Carl likes this place

SUDHAUS Kassel
Hafenstrasse 54, 34125
+49 (0)561 9979 7470
mail@sudhaus-kassel.de
www.sudhaus-kassel.de
Tram: Platz der Deutschen Einheit
Carl likes this place

Vinobar Il Teatro
Oberste Gasse 11, 34117
+49 (0)561 287 2674
Facebook @vinobarilteatro
Tram: Königsplatz
Oliver likes this place

Weinbergkrug
Frankfurterstrasse 54, 34121
+49 (0)561 8164 8366
kassel@weinbergkrug.com
www.weinberg-kafe.de
www.weinbergkrug.de
Tram: Am Weinberg
Carmen and Susanne like this place

Shopping

Antiquariat & Verlag Winfried Jenior
Books
Marienstrasse 5, 34117
+49 (0)561 739 1621
info@jenior.de
www.jenior.de
Tram: Weigelstrasse
Carmen likes this place

Perlenrausch
Quirky jewellery and documenta artist
Zentgrafenstrasse 142, 34130
+49 (0)561 6029 3526
schmuck@im-perlenrausch.de
www.im-perlenrausch.de
Tram: Kirche Kirchditmold
Carl likes this place

Rotopol
Illustrated books and art
Friedrich-Ebert-Strasse 95, 34119
+49 (0)561 630 5583
info@rotopol.de
www.rotopol.de
Tram: Querallee
Carmen likes this place

soki store
Upcycling fashion
Friedrich-Ebert-Strasse 101, 34119
+49 (0)561 5034 8873
info@soki-kassel.de
www.soki-kassel.de
Tram: Querallee
Kira and Sophie like this place

Weinhandlung Bremer
Alcohol
Friedrich-Ebert-Strasse 61, 34117
+49 (0)561 766 8332
kassel@weinhandlung-bremer.de
www.weinhandlung-bremer.de
Tram: Karthäuserstrasse
Carl likes this place

WIKULLiL
Stationery
Frankfurter Strasse 58, 34121
+49 (0)561 9895 2636
info@wikullil.com
www.wikullil.com
Tram: Am Weinberg
Carmen likes this place

Wildwood Gallery & Store
Concept store and gallery
Friedrich-Ebert-Strasse 99, 34119
+49 (0)561 9201 9949
info@wild-wood.de
www.wild-wood.de
Tram: Querallee
Carl likes this place

Places to visit

Aschrottpark
Outdoor space
34119, Tram: Wintershall
Oliver likes this place

Auestadion
Sports stadium
Damaschkestrasse 1, 34121
+49 (0)561 25 474
info@ksv-hessen.de
www.ksvhessen.de
Tram: Auestadion
Khesrau and Sohrab like this place

Bali cinema
Independent cinema
KulturBahnhof Kassel, Rainer-
Dierichs-Platz 1, 34117
+49 (0)561 71 0550
info@balikinos.de
www.balikinos.de
Train: Kassel Hauptbahnhof
Carmen and Susanne like this place

Bergpark Wilhelmshöhe
**Park, Schloss Wilhelmshöhe
palace, Hercules statue, Glass
House and Water Games**
Schlosspark 1, 34131
+49(0)561 3168 0123
besucherdienst@museum-kassel.de
www.museum-kassel.de
www.beleuchtete-wasserspiele.de
Tram: Wilhelmshöhe (Park)
*Kazuo, Khesrau, Sohrab, Kira,
Sophie and Oliver like this place*

Blue Dancer
Art installation over Fulda river
Die Schlagd, 34123
Tram: Altmarkt/
Regierungspräsidium
Kazuo likes this

Brasselsberg
Neighbourhood
34132
Bus: Brasselsberg
*Khesrau, Sohrab and Oliver like
this place*

Diakonie Kliniken
Creation art installation
Herkulesstrasse 34, 34119
+49 (0)561 10 020
www.diako-kassel.de
Tram: Kirchweg
Kazuo likes this place

Die Galerien
Gallery
Frankfurter Strasse 54, 34121
info@galerien-kassel.de
www.galerien-kassel.de
Tram: Am Weinberg
Carl likes this place

Filmladen cinema
Independent cinema
Goethestrasse 31, 34119
+49 (0)561 707 650
info@filmladen.de
www.filmladen.de
Tram: Goethestrasse
Carmen and Susanne like this place

Friedrich-Ebert-Strasse
Street
34119
Tram: Querallee
*Khesrau, Sohrab, Kira and Sophie
like this place*

Fridericianum
Contemporary art museum
Friedrichplatz 18, 34117
+49 (0)561 707 2720
info@fridericianum.org
www.fridericianum.org
Tram: Friedrichplatz
*Kira, Sophie, Oliver and Susanne
like this place*

Fuldaaue and Fulda river
**Outdoor space and Bugasee
lake**
34123
Tram: Bahnhof Niederzwehren
*Carmen, Kazuo and Oliver like
this place*

Gemäldegalerie Alte Meister
Art gallery
Schloss Wilhelmshöhe,
Schlosspark 1, 34131
info@museum-kassel.de
www.museum-kassel.de
Tram: Wilhelmshöhe (Park)
Oliver and Susanne like this place

Gloria cinema
Independent cinema
Friedrich-Ebert-Strasse, 34117
+49 (0)561 766 7950
info@balikinos.de
www.balikinos.de
Tram: Karthäuserstrasse
Carmen and Susanne like this place

Goetheanlage
Outdoor space
34119
Tram: Wintershall
Oliver likes this place

Goldgrube Kassel
Music venue
Eisenschmiede 85, 34127
Facebook @goldgrubekassel
Tram: Hauptfriedhof
Carl likes this place

International Minimal Music Festival
www.minimal-music-festival.de
Susanne likes this

Karlsaue Park
Outdoor space
34121
Tram: Heinrich-Heine-Strasse/
Universität
*Carmen, Kazuo, Khesrau, Sohrab,
Kira, Sophie, Oliver and Susanne
like this place*

Kasseler Berge autobahn A7
Mountains and view over city
34355
*Khesrau, Sohrab and Oliver like
this place*

Kasseler Kunstverein
Art space
Friedrichsplatz 18, 34117
+49 (0)561 771 169
info@kasselerkunstverein.de
www.kasselerkunstverein.de
Tram: Friedrichsplatz
Susanne likes this place

Königsstrasse
Street and square
34117
Tram: Königsplatz
Oliver likes this place

Kulturzentrum Schlachthof
Cultural centre
Mombachstrasse 12, 34127
+49 (0)561 983 500
info@schlachthof-kassel.de
www.schlachthof-kassel.de
Tram: Mombachstrasse
Carmen likes this place

Kunsttempel
Art space
Friedrich-Ebert-Strasse 177, 34119
+49 (0)561 24 304
www.kunsttempel.net
Tram: Kongress Palais /
Stadthalle
Carmen likes this place

Kurbad Jungborn
Bathtub museum
Sternstrasse 22, 34123
+49 (0)561 65 785
kontakt@kurbad-jungborn.de
www.kurbad-jungborn.de
Tram: Altmarkt
Carmen likes this place

Kurhessen Therme
Spa
Wilhelmshöher Allee 361, 34131
+49 (0)561 318 080
info@kurhessen-therme.de
www.kurhessen-therme.de
Tram: Kurhessen-Therme
Khesrau and Sohrab like this place

LAGE
Art gallery
Elfbuchenstrasse 20, 34119
hi@lage-kassel.de
www.lage-kassel.de
Tram: Friedenskirche
Susanne likes this pace

Laserscape
documenta 6 installation
Karl-Bernhardi-Strasse, 34117
Tram: Friedrichsplatz
Oliver likes this

Natural History Museum
Steinweg 2, 34117
+49 (0)561 787 4066
naturkundemuseum@kassel.de
www.naturkundemuseum-kassel.de
Tram: Friedrichsplatz
Oliver likes this place

Neue Galerie
Art gallery
Schöne Aussicht 1, 34117
+49 (0)561 3168 0400
info@museum-kassel.de
www.museum-kassel.de
Tram: Rathaus
Kazuo and Susanne like this place

SOZO visions in motion
Dance company
Grüner Weg 15–17, 34117
+49 (0)561 937 2858
info@sozo-vim.de
www.sozo-vim.de
Tram: Lutherplatz
Carmen likes this place

St. Martin's Church
Organ with hair
Martinsplatz 5a, 34117
+49 (0)561 9200 0919
info@musik-martinskirche.de
www.musik-martinskirche.de
Tram: Am Stern
Susanne likes this place

Staatstheater Kassel
Theatre
Friedrichsplatz 15, 34117
+49 (0)561 109 40
www.staatstheater-kassel.de
Tram: Friedrichsplatz
*Kira, Sophie and Oliver like this
place*

The Vertical Earth Kilometer
documenta 6 installation
Friedrichsplatz Park, 34117
Tram: Friedrichsplatz
Susanne likes this

Theaterstübchen
Art and culture venue
Jordanstrasse 11, 34117
+49 (0)561 816 5706
www.theaterstuebchen.de
Tram: Ständeplatz
Carmen likes this place

Tokonoma
Art space
Frankfurterstrasse 58, 34121
info@supertokonoma.de
www.supertokonoma.de
Tram: Am Weinberg
Carmen and Susanne like this place

Werkstätten Brandthaus
Scale modelling hub
Erzbergerstrasse 49, 34117
+49 (0)56 1804 3488
www.werkstattbrandthaus.com/
kontakt.html
Tram: Lutherplatz
Kazuo likes this place

Useful websites

FRIZZ:
www.frizz-kassel.de
Kazuo likes this

Entrepreneurial Kassel

Here are our favourite entrepreneurial and creative initiatives in the city of Kassel.

KulturBahnhof
When Kassel-Wilhelmshöhe train station opened in the 1990s, the importance of Kassel Hauptbahnhof for travel declined. An initiative to turn the station into a predominantly cultural hub followed. Nowadays, there are new artistic initiatives happening there all the time. Of particular interest is the decommissioned railway track which became a *documenta 10* artwork, as well as the Caricatura museum, and the cultural space Nachrichtenmeisterei around the corner.
Rainer Dierichs Platz 1, 34117
+49 (0)561 739 9011
thoener@kulturbahnhof-kassel.de
www.kulturbahnhof-kassel.de
Train: Kassel Hauptbahnhof

Bike Tyson
The bicycle entrepreneur who runs this shop restores, repairs and sells vintage racing cycles. If you're planning on staying in Kassel for a little while and want to get around in true style, this is the place for you.
Bettenhäuser Strasse 10, 34123
+49 (0)151 4001 4482
info@biketyson.de
www.biketyson.de
Tram: Unterneustädter Kirchplatz

Mr. Wilson
One of the oldest skateboarding and roller sports clubs in Germany, Mr. Wilson supports youth culture and creative expression with an anti-establishment undertone.

It's a place to get involved in activities, while the less active can kick back at Café Libre. Mr. Wilson is in the Rothenditmold creative district, home to many artists, musicians and design ateliers in and around the old spinning mill.
Brandausstrasse 1-3, 34127
+49 (0)561 2879 0791
info@mister-wilson.de
www.kesselschmie.de
Train: Kassel Hauptbahnhof

Nextkassel
This is a citizen laboratory where locals work with planners and designers to create a city vision for Kassel. A range of innovative ideas for the city are available to view on the Nextkassel website, from artistic designs of underpasses to a 'Casselfornia' leisure park. There are occasional events to discuss ideas further too.
www.nextkassel.de

Kleine-Freiheit-Camper
The entrepreneurial owner of Kleine-Freiheit-Camper transforms normal vans into little campers, perfect for road trips. Each camper van comes fully equipped with everything you need for a camper van trip, including a solar panel on the roof and a hammock ready to be tied between two trees in your ideal location. Those tempted to embark on a road trip following a Kassel visit will be sure to travel in style.
www.kleine-freiheit-camper.de

Aust & Amelung
This design duo create furniture, interiors and exhibition architecture. They've won several awards and are included in various permanent collections around the world, such as the Shanghai Museum of Glass. See their *like paper* concrete pendant lamp in the restaurant Voit, or their *KasselKino* interior at Stadtmuseum Kassel. They also won the design.work. space competition in 2014 for the interior concept of the co-working space at Science Park Kassel.
www.aust-amelung.com

Stadtimkerei Kassel
This city beekeeping initiative embodies the entrepreneurial spirit of local produce while helping the environment. Permanent beehive stands can be found across the city, from Weinberg in the centre of Kassel and the rooftop of the Kulturbunker in west Kassel, to the Dönche Nature Reserve and near the banks of the Fulda river in the eastern neighbourhood, Unterneustadt. The honey is different every year, depending on the weather, which plants thrive during each season and the time of harvest. Among other things, the honey is used to brew craftBEE beer (p14).
www.stadtimkerei-kassel.de

Photo: Kleine-Freiheit-Camper

Photos: Weinberg Ecke

Weinberg Corner

Weinberg Corner (Weinberg Ecke) consists of four different spaces which have all made a name for themselves in their own right. Kafe NEU Am Weinberg is for lunch, afternoon coffee and cake, wine and records, with special events such as folk/jazz/indie concerts, readings and talks. Weinbergkrug is for drinking and being merry to the backdrop of DJ sets, trash concerts or karaoke. IDEAL is a gallery, art collective and occasional cinema, while Warte Für Kunst is a gallery, private meeting space and dining room. It's easy to see why this is a hotspot for Kasselaners who love anything and everything creative and entrepreneurial. The spaces are run by Canadian musician and Kassel local Craig Bjerring (*Oldseed*) and his friends; Craig also regularly tours solo across the world. This is a place not to be missed in Kassel.

Frankfurter Strasse 54, 34121
Facebook @weinberg.kafe @weinbergkrug @idealverein
www.warte-kunst.de
Tram: Am Weinberg

Kira Kimm and Sophie Roscher

Upcycling fashion entrepreneurs

These sustainable fashion designers are born and bred Kasselaners. After training as tailors for the theatre and going on to experience unethical practices of major fashion brands, they set up their own upcycling fashion label. soki is the first sustainable fashion brand in Kassel, and co-founders Kira and Sophie have gained notoriety in fashion and entrepreneurial circles for their designs, and for their philosophy on sustainable fashion.

Introduce yourselves.

Sophie: I'm the 'so' of soki! Kira and I were both born and raised in Kassel and we met each other when we were 16 years old. Our friends and families still live in Kassel and we have always felt very comfortable in our home town.

Kira: I'm the 'ki' of soki! Both Sophie and I enjoyed sewing since we were kids, and we eventually turned our hobby into our profession. After finishing school, we undertook a three-year professional training programme to become tailors at the Staatstheater Kassel.

How would your friends describe you?
Sophie: We've always been known as the DIY-girls, who are creative and love to sew.

Why is Kassel a good place to set up a business?
Sophie: So far, our business idea is unique in Kassel and the city is open to new and creative ideas like ours.
Kira: We also wanted to stay in our home town because we love living here, with friends and family nearby.

Tell us about how your business started.
Kira: After completing our training to become tailors, we didn't want to contribute to unsustainable conditions within the fashion industry. For a very short time, I worked for a company whose garments were produced in terrible conditions in Bangladesh. I quickly knew I didn't want to be part of this.
Sophie: We sat down together and thought about alternative approaches to incorporate our philosophy of sustainable, fair fashion. Over a glass of red wine, we decided to create something special. And so our fashion label, soki, was born.

Which Kassel neighbourhood did you start your business in?
Kira: We set up a studio at my parents' home and immediately implemented our upcycling mission by sewing boxer shorts from old bedsheets! We designed two collections, which we sold in four stores in Kassel. We got a lot of positive feedback straight away. Showing what could be done with old bed linen really captured peoples' imaginations.
Sophie: Soon, space became tight in our small workshop, so we found a shop with a lot of space and opened our soki store in April 2016. We sew everything together and work hard to keep our physical and online shops stocked up. In addition to our own collections, we sell sustainable products from other labels. We're a green concept store offering many options for sustainable living.

Which Kassel neighbourhood do you live and work in?
Sophie: We both live in our own apartments in west Kassel, which is the most beautiful part of Kassel. It's great there are so many nice small shops, cafés and restaurants in the area. It's also very central, so we can travel anywhere by bike.
Kira: Our soki store is also located in west Kassel, so our commute to work is very short! We're surrounded by many small, independent shops like ours. There's also an increasing number of creative people with great ideas coming to this part of town. We're very glad to have our store on the popular Friedrich-Ebert-Strasse and we're curious about all the new things yet to come to the area.

What do your customers most love about soki clothing?
Kira: Our customers have the opportunity to participate in the design process by selecting the bed linen themselves before a piece of clothing is created. So when they buy a piece of soki clothing, no-one else in the entire world has it.

Tell us about the upcycling trend.
Sophie: Upcycling is the most sustainable method to create fair clothing: no new resources are needed and less waste is generated. Before any old garment is thrown away, we will always make a new piece of clothing out of it. We sew one-of-a-kind pieces which can be purchased with a clear conscience.

Kira: We're very glad people are showing more interest in sustainable lifestyles. Many people find it surprising what wonderful things can be done with old bed sheets! From the fashion perspective, the limited amount of fabric we have means we can guarantee everyone gets a piece of clothing no-one else is wearing.

Where is your favourite place to work?

Sophie: For us, there's no better place to work than in the soki store. We love our store and our workshop, and we have everything we need there.

Kira: Since we're open all day, there's no other workplace we'd have the opportunity to go to anyway, and we usually have lunch in our store. On the rare occasions we're able to go out for lunch, we choose a nice restaurant nearby. Sapori at the Bebelplatz is a favourite of ours and it's a good place to discuss business over excellent food.

Where do you find inspiration in Kassel?

Kira: There's no single place we get inspiration for our work. Many ideas come to us spontaneously. Taking walks surrounded by nature can spark ideas, and the Karlsaue Park or Bergpark with its large Hercules monument are great places for this. Kassel also has some inspirational museums such as the Fridericianum.

Sophie: We can be inspired in many places, be it at home, in the store, with friends or at events. The funny thing is that we usually have the same ideas!

Describe the feeling in Kassel when *documenta* is on.

Sophie: During *documenta*, there's a lot going on in Kassel. You suddenly see a lot of enthusiastic tourists and Kassel becomes the centre of the world for 100 days.

Kira: As locals, it gives us the opportunity to look at something interesting every day and to get to know art from across the world.

What sound do you associate with Kassel?

Sophie: The sound of Kassel is very obvious: *Milky Chance*. They're now world famous musicians but they also grew up in Kassel. We're very proud of our boys!

Do entrepreneurs experience the city differently from other Kassel locals?

Kira: Since we became entrepreneurs ourselves, we do experience the city differently. We're always surprised, very happy and extremely proud to see people around Kassel with our soki clothes on. After all, we held each piece of clothing in our hands, and we know exactly who made what at which moment in time.

Sophie: As hands-on business owners, we also meet many new people every day, whether it's customers who come to our store, or other self-employed people and business owners from the neighbourhood. From time to time, we appear in local newspaper articles and television reports, so gaining a bit of popularity makes our experience of Kassel different too.

Where's your favourite place for a coffee?

Kira: You can get a really good cappuccino at Café Melchior or Rokkeberg, which are both in west Kassel.

Sophie: We love cappuccino! But unfortunately, we often lack the time to go to a café.

Where are your favourite places for a meal out in Kassel?

Sophie: At the moment, our favourite place to eat is the Vietnamese restaurant Pho Vang, which is in the city centre. There are also many foodie delicacies to be found in our neighbourhood, such as the Indian restaurant Bashis Delight and the sushi restaurant, Shinyu.

Kira: The market hall in the city centre also offers great possibilities to eat delicious food. In particular, we love Kleine Kantine and Ahlemächt'jer. Both places are run by friends of ours who have created wonderful independent eateries.

Where do you like going for a drink?

Kira: For a glass of wine, beer or a fine cocktail we like to go to the Caricatura Bar, Fes or King Schulz.

What is the current trend in Kassel?

Sophie: We're very pleased that the trend to live and consume more sustainably and consciously has reached Kassel. Especially in the west Kassel neighbourhood, this lifestyle has already existed for a longer time. Healthy and regional organic products, sustainable clothing and more environmental awareness are highly valued and appreciated here. Of course, we hope this trend will last and become even bigger.

How would you advise visitors to Kassel to blend in and live like the locals do?

Kira: One important piece of advice to Kassel visitors is not to freak out when you meet the guys of *Milky Chance* in the supermarket. Yes, they are some of the few super-famous people here, but we think it's kind of embarrassing to freak out when you see them walking around in their home town.

Kira: Also, you should not be super friendly in Kassel. Being a bit rough is unfortunately typical for Kasselaners!

Sophie: And be sure to get yourself an Ahle Worscht, which is a type of salami, because this is a specialty from Kassel!

What do you do at the weekend?

Sophie: On Saturdays our store is open from 11:00 to 15:00. After that, we have to do the things we didn't get done during the week, such as cleaning our apartments and doing the food shopping. In the evening, we always look forward to a good party, cooking with friends or a delicious drink in a bar.

Kira: Sunday is our only free day, so this means it's time for rest and relaxation! We sleep in, have breakfast in bed, do yoga and visit family or friends. And sometimes we also treat ourselves to a small weekend trip! Sometimes we go for city breaks, or spend relaxing weekends by the North Sea with our boyfriends.

Where's the best place to soak up the feeling of Kassel?

Sophie: Taking a walk on Friedrich-Ebert-Strasse is great because it's buzzing and great for people-watching.

Kira: Don't forget to visit our soki store when you go there!

Find out more about soki at www.soki-kassel.de

chapter 4

Getting away and getting lost

*Wandering aimlessly without a plan
sometimes brings unexpected inspiration.*

Away for a day

Get away from the city for a day with outdoorsy adventures in the areas surrounding Kassel.

Sababurg

This district less than an hour north of Kassel is most famous for its Sleeping Beauty Castle. Named after the Brothers Grimm fairy tale, the ruins of this hill castle are magical to explore. It's an apt place to visit, given the connection the Grimm brothers had with Kassel and the region in general. Part of the ruins were restored in the 1950s to create a hotel. This is a great place to stop for lunch before getting out on foot and exploring the castle ruins. The Sababurg Wildlife Park is below the castle; watching bison graze with the castle in the background is an inspiring sight.
www.sababurg.de
Transport: Catch the train from Kassel Hauptbahnhof to Hofgeismar, then take bus 190 to Sababurg.

Edersee

Just over an hour south-west of Kassel is one of the largest lakes in Europe, the 27km long man-made Edersee. Ideal for summertime day trips, visit the Edersee to try your hand at a range of water sports, or take a hike in the 15,000 acre UNESCO Kellerwald-Edersee National Park, the largest connected wood rush and beech forest complex in Central Europe. For relaxing days out, a refreshing swim followed by a picnic on the riverbank is idyllic. For yet more indulgence, a visit to one of the spa hotels such as Hotel Freund is just what the doctor ordered.
www.edersee.com
Transport: Catch the 500 bus from Kassel Hauptbahnhof, then take bus 510 to Ederseebahn-Radweg.

Willingen

This locality under two hours west of Kassel is a lush forested area ideal for a total change of scenery. Best known for winter sports, spend a day skiing at Skigebiet Willingen. There are 18km of slopes for different abilities, ski schools, toboggan runs, and plenty of opportunities for après ski in various bars. Keen spectators should go to Willingen for the International Ski Federation's annual World Cup ski-jumping competition. The Willingen area is also popular for mountain biking and hiking.
www.willingen.de
Transport: Take the train from Kassel-Wilhelmshöhe to Brilon Wald, then take the train to Willingen.

Away for a weekend

Discover more of what Germany has to offer entrepreneurs and creatives during a weekend away.

Frankfurt

One of the closest larger cities to Kassel at less than an hour and a half away, Frankfurt is far from being just a global financial centre. During the summer, the city comes alive with deckchair-clad man-made beaches and riverside festivals. During the rest of the year too, there are foodie events, flea markets to get lost in, and independent coffee roasteries to discover, such as Kaffeerösterei Wissmüller tucked away in a courtyard. The city loves a pop-up too, with collaborations taking place such as Showmanship, the city's first natural wine bar in a centuries-old castle in the Alt-Sachsenhausen neighbourhood.

www.frankfurt-tourismus.de

Transport: Catch the train from Kassel-Wilhelmshöhe to Frankfurt (Main) Hauptbahnhof.

Leipzig

Around three hours from the centre of Kassel is Germany's emerging hotspot for art, culture and creativity. Leipzig has a start-up scene that's materialising with some force and a free-spirited attitude to being creative and putting ideas into practice. A visit to Leipzig is all about soaking up the positivity created by the entrepreneurs and creatives of the city. Visit the co-working hub Raumstation, explore the major arts centre Leipziger Baumwollspinnerei – full of artist studios and galleries, and check out the city's many café/bar/art projects such as Dr. Seltsam.

www.carlgoes.com/leipzig

www.leipzig.travel

Transport: Catch the train from Kassel-Wilhelmshöhe to Fulda, then take the train to Leipzig Hauptbahnhof.

East Frisian Islands

When Kasselaners feel like a weekend by the sea, heading to the North Sea is the closest option. Going a little bit further by catching a ferry to any of the East Frisian Islands is an ideal option for getting away from it all; it takes around six hours to get from Kassel to the islands. Visit the busiest islands of Borkum or Norderney for the watersport-packed sandy beaches and a bustling cultural calendar. Or head to the car-free islands for a more peaceful weekend. Juist, known as Magic Land (Töwerland) by locals, has an art trail on Otto Leege Path, thalassotherapy and a lively springtime music festival. The island also looks set to be the world's first carbon-neutral tourism destination by 2030.

www.niedersachsen-tourism.com

Transport: Catch the train from Kassel-Wilhelmshöhe to Bremen Hauptbahnhof, then take the train to Norddeich Mole. From there, catch the ferry to the island of your choice.

Away forever

Sometimes it's time to say goodbye. Here are our tips for where Kassel fans should head to next.

Berlin

When Kassel's creatives and start-up entrepreneurs decide they want to leave Kassel, it's Frankfurt or Berlin they head to. Berlin – a city jam-packed with start-up scenesters and artsy creatives – has an obvious appeal. With outdoor spaces big and small, the city has a green feeling Kasselaners are accustomed to, while spending summertimes by the river with a beer in hand is practically the law. There's a creative project to get to know on every corner, and a festival or cultural happening most days of the week. Unlike in Kassel, co-working is a huge trend in Berlin, with like-minded people working, networking and socialising together. Mixing in its unique history and post- Berlin Wall pioneering spirit, Berlin is an intoxicating city to call home for a while.

www.carlgoes.com/berlin
www.visitberlin.de

Basel

This Swiss city is marginally smaller than Kassel, and comes highly respected in the art world. Indeed, art lovers flock to the city during the summer for the Art Basel market weekend that sees creativity peak. Aside from this, the city is home to revered museums with long histories and contemporary art projects, with Kunsthalle Basel especially prominent. Basel is home to innovation in other areas too, with start-up academies, accelerators and inspiring co-working spaces. Basel also has a solid sense of design, and the Vitra Design Museum is on the city outskirts. With the Rhine river running through the city, guarded by old buildings housing traditional and modern businesses, Basel is up there when it comes to inspiration.

www.basel.com

Athens

documenta organisers formed a link between Kassel and Athens for *documenta 14*, making it a natural next step from Kassel for those interested in the art world. Indeed, artistic ventures abound in the Greek city, from the Kunsthalle Athena art centre, to small artist studios in unexpected spots such as Egg Studio. It's not just an art city though. Athens is home to a thriving start-up scene and co-working spaces abound, the largest of which are Impact Hub and The Cube. While the city is busier and faster-paced than Kassel, with less green space too, the city is nevertheless home to plenty of spots to explore and unwind. Just like Kassel, it's a place where people from many other parts of the world come together and put their vision into practice. That's intriguing enough for us.

www.visitgreece.gr

Getting lost

Wandering without having a destination in mind is becoming a lost art in cities today. Paying no attention to street names and directions, the ticking of time and 'having a plan', is a liberating way to enjoy a moment in time.

'Getting lost' is not a new concept. Flâneurs — idle strollers — were first talked about in the 16th century. A concept with no exact English translation, flânerie is all about aimless wandering, losing yourself and urban exploration.

We urge you to get lost in Kassel and experience the rhythm of the city without thought or direction. Our suggestions are simply starting points for the adventures you'll create. Whether you decide to jump on a tram and travel six stops, or make a spontaneous beeline for something that looks interesting, it's up to you.

Wandering aimlessly without a plan sometimes brings unexpected inspiration. We challenge you to give it a try.

1. Clear your mind in Kassel's abundant green spaces and discover documenta installations from times past, such as in Karlsaue Park and Bergpark Wilhelmshöhe.
2. Discover Papiercafé, tucked away in Art University Kassel for coffee, cool books and creative space.
3. Stroll along Lange Strasse near Kassel-Wilhelmshöhe station, for the quaint feeling of a Kassel from the olden days.

Photo: Stephan Kaiser © Stadt Kassel

Photo: Papiercafé

Photo: Sasha Arms